Ping Pong Gold Medal Edition

TAHL LEIBOVITZ

PING PONG FOR FIGHTERS

ISBN:1541376196
ISBN-13:978-1541376199

DEDICATION

For my wife of more than 10 years and the real Champion, Dawn Leibovitz.

CONTENTS

"The most important thing in the Olympic Games is not to win but to take part, just as the most important thing in life is not the triumph, but the struggle. The essential thing is not to have conquered, but to have fought well." – The Olympic Creed

UPDATE

It's been more than two years since I wrote Ping Pong For Fighters. The book has done exceptionally well. I am glad that so many people have had the chance to read this material. What you are reading now is the Gold Medal Edition of Ping Pong For Fighters. So, what is different about this book as compared to Ping Pong For Fighters? I have read the original version of Ping Pong For Fighters many times and received a tremendous amount of feedback about the book from many different readers.

In 'Ping Pong for Fighters Gold Medal Edition' I have removed two small sections from the book because I felt that they took away from the flow of the book. I also added two extra chapters at the end of the book mostly because I have received many emails from people asking about my experiences at the 2015 Para Pan Am Games as well as the 2016 Rio Paralympics.

I am now completely satisfied with this version of Ping Pong For Fighters; it is even more clear and concise than the first edition. I believe the reader will gain a tremendous amount of insight from the additional chapters I have added to this book. I want to thank you for purchasing this book. I hope you enjoy reading it as much as I did writing it.

Tahl Leibovitz MA, LMSW

Paralympic Gold Medalist

FORWARD

Fifty years ago, I made a decision. I wanted to become a table tennis player. I was twelve years old. The Swedish and the Japanese teams were training in my hometown Falkenberg. I spent time in the hall whenever I wasn't in school. To see them practice was so inspiring. I wanted to be like them.

In 1968 I was invited to a training camp with 12-time world champion Mr. Ichiro Ogimura, who was in Sweden. A year later I got to travel to Japan to train under him. He changed my life. What he taught me has been the basis for my table tennis career as a player and a coach, as well as a human being. In three and a half months I changed my whole game. One year later at seventeen, I became professional.

It has been a fantastic journey. To have your hobby as your job is great. It doesn't feel like work even though I trained harder than most. I have played against every World Champion from 1963 to 1993 - an amazing group of players. I have coached many players who have had great success on many different levels.

Tahl Leibovitz, the author of this book, has the talent that matches any of the world champions I've coached. I met Tahl for the first time seven years ago when the US National Para Team had a training camp in San Diego. I realized rather quickly that he was a great player. What he can do with the ball is amazing. His variation of spin, speed and placement is outstanding. Not only that, he has the knowledge of table tennis that matches any of the champions. He has a fantastic understanding of the game.

Any player can profit from this great book. It gives you an insight of the secrets of table tennis. By following the tips and advice, your game will take a giant leap.

Enjoy the game and good luck,

Stellan Bengtsson

INTRODUCTION

My name is Tahl Leibovitz. I am 39 years old. I have been playing table tennis for 25 years. I'm also a Paralympic gold medalist.

Over the years, I've found that knowledge is one of the main things separating average players from good players, and good players from the great. I thought it'd be cool if the average table tennis player could know what the best players know and also how they think. There are many excellent table tennis books out there with great technical instruction, but I found there's more to the sport than just technique. Knowledge is vital. If you know more about the sport and what the great players do, you can play better.

This book is called *Ping Pong for Fighters*, and it's about fighting all the different elements that are attached to table tennis. The fight starts inward and eventually moves outward: from within ourselves, to the ball, to our opponents, to the environment. I've found that most people lose because they choose to fight against themselves without focusing on the other elements as well. Hence to improve,

We have to know our environment.
We have to know the opponent.
We have to know the ball.
We have to know ourselves.

In *Ping Pong For Fighters*, you will find a philosophy I've developed based on observing high-level players and coaches, as well as my own experience in the sport - over 20 years of international and domestic competition. While reading this book, you might experience a side of table tennis that's very different from what you might have seen before. The goal of this book is to help you see more possibilities in table tennis and help you to approach the sport in a different way. You will learn how to identify and deal with the frustrations that come with table tennis and learn how you can find immense enjoyment from the sport of table tennis.

I think this book will teach us about the importance of competing and how we need to keep on battling regardless of who we're playing. My best matches have occurred when I went into battle. I wasn't convinced I would win and I wasn't sure I would lose. I was ready for the challenge, and that is what this book is about.

I hope to encourage the average table tennis player to look at table tennis differently. It's the approach to the sport that we should be most concerned about, and that is what I hope we can explore with this book. I hope that everyone who plays the sport of table tennis can use what is written here to see more of the possibilities within us.

Finally, before we begin, I want to thank you for purchasing this book. I have been working on it for almost six years now, and I am extremely satisfied with how it all came together. I am currently attending the NYU Silver School of Social Work and will be graduating with a Master of Social Work in May 2015. The proceeds from this book will make it possible for me to attend school, complete my final year of graduate school, and support my family. Thank you again for your help and good luck in your table tennis journey.

Fight hard, and never give up.

Tahl Leibovitz

1 THE FIGHT AGAINST THE ENVIRONMENT

Prologue: Welcome To Hell

Team USA was sent to a Para Tournament in Argentina a few years ago, we were crammed into a tiny bus, alongside players from other countries. I remember being very physically uncomfortable during the entire ride due to sitting for so long. Eight hours later, we arrived at the playing hall, or rather, what was supposed to be a playing hall

The tournament was held literally inside a giant shed. It was December, freezing, and I'm walking around the place with a heavy winter jacket. There was no heat, and water dripped down onto the tables. Garbage pails collected water that was literally pouring from the ceiling in many places. I played most of my matches wearing a sweatshirt.

And during that tournament I played exceptionally well.

Most of the players became so frustrated that they were simply unable to compete. I soon realized that I could choose to see the obstacles in a negative way, or be positive. Sure, the conditions in Argentina were terrible, but we all had to play in the same conditions anyway. I found I could perform better as long as I remained neutral and focused on the things within my control.

You Are Not In Control

Samuel Jackson has a great line in *The Negotiator* - "YOU ARE NOT IN CONTROL".

Many table tennis players including myself arrive at tournaments with mental baggage, allowing distractions to affect the way we play. But what we often don't realize is that most of these things are beyond our control, tournament conditions, waiting times for matches, how well our opponent has trained for the match. These things are not in our control!

The key here is to learn which factors are within our control and which factors are not. Once we're able to do that, we can then get into the right competitive mindset without being distracted, being able to focus on the things we actually have control over. Going with another water example, should we be angry if we get caught in a rainstorm? Perhaps. Maybe we could have avoided being soaked if we had checked the weather forecast beforehand.

But should we get angry just because it rains?

While there are many things we can't control in table tennis, we *can* prevent ourselves from being affected and overwhelmed by them. We can't choose how many nets or edges our opponents get, but we can choose to stay calm and not show our frustration. This is something I've been working on constantly throughout my career. When I think positively, I play at my best. We may not be able to dictate the outcome of a match, but we can control our training prior to the match, whether we get enough sleep the night before and our state of mind as we play. We have no control over the weather outside, but we can choose whether we go out into the rain with our rain gear on.

Approaching a Match

What is a tournament? What is a table tennis match? Contrary to popular belief, a tournament is not a place to win and lose matches. Instead, think of a tournament as *an arena for competition*. If I walk into a tournament fixated on my results, the prize money, or how I can impress others with my performance, then I have misunderstood the tournament's purpose. The tournament is a platform where we compete, and our actions should be aligned with just that - the idea of competition. Before a tournament, we prepare to compete. And once the day arrives, we should be focused on battling our opponent, nothing else.

Every match is 50-50. Keep telling yourself that. Every match is a new event, a new day of competition. For most top players, one of the secrets to winning is to approach every match like a battle. Sure, some of us are simply not competitive people by nature, or we might regard table tennis as more of a recreational and social activity used to relieve stress. That is perfectly fine. But regardless of who you are or your reasons for playing table tennis, possessing the mindset of "I'm here to compete" helps gives you the belief that you can match up to the person on the opposite side of the table. By focusing on the battle at hand, you'll be able to avoid being distracted and frustrated by things outside your control. You'll be able to play positively, and before you know it, give yourself a chance at victory.

Also, while we do not focus on winning or losing, we should have the self-belief that we can win. We should be comfortable with seeing ourselves on the podium wearing the gold medal. We should be comfortable with winning. We should know that we have the capability to win. Winning should not be a shock to us.

Besides an arena for competition, think of a table tennis game as a series of decision-making opportunities. Each point is an event where decisions are presented to us. Having more opportunities to put the ball where we want helps us make better decisions. As table tennis players, we must learn when to take what shot and how.

These choices could be diminished in a match. For example, if your opponent puts the ball to your forehand and you're only able to place the ball down the line or cross-court, you have less choices and chances to play the ball where you desire.

There are a few reasons for this. Firstly, it could be technical inabilities caused by bad stroke mechanics or footwork. Another could be the previous placement on the last ball played, allowing my opponent to put me in a poor position. Finally, it could be my limited knowledge, not knowing that I can utilize better positions when it comes to my own ball placement.

The solution to all these things? Practice. Make sure you can play the ball to various locations on the table when you are attacking or blocking. Can you loop the ball deep? Can you loop the ball to your opponent's wide forehand, middle, backhand, forehand and wide backhand from your middle? Can you change the depth of the ball? In other words, try and make sure you can put the ball to multiple locations on the table when you are playing with your backhand or forehand.

Medals are Won or Lost in the Village

There's this running joke in the Olympic and Paralympic community about how medals are won and lost in the Village. How we conduct ourselves in the Village determines to a great extent our ability to compete during the Games themselves. Every action we take in the village is a reflection of how we behave during our competition matches.

Some Olympians and Paralympians have already accepted a pre-determined outcome before they start competing. The same thing may happen in our matches. We can also harm ourselves before we even play. We sometimes tell ourselves that specific things have to occur or we have to feel a certain way prior to the match in order to play our very best. This approach to competing is not based in reality and can hinder our performance instead!

While it is good to draw on past successes to get into a more positive state of mind, needing to go through a specific sequence of events just to play well might not be ideal. For example, many players tell themselves that they have to hit the ball a certain way during the warm-up to "feel good". The truth is you don't need some sort of pre-match ritual in order to do well. Good players know you don't just go out and start playing amazing. Playing your best is a gradual process that occurs throughout the match.

Remember that what you do before and after the match can directly affect the match performance itself.

The tournament match, in its entirety, is played in three phases: before the match, during the match and after the match. And if we're not careful, harmful thinking can occur in any one of these three.

Focus on the things that can prepare us properly for the match. Do we need 10 minutes of warm up? Do we need to stretch a little more? Do we need to reassess our mental game? Don't let external circumstances dictate how you will play! If something is not directly relevant to our performance, we should never let it become a factor in our competition.

Your Past Doesn't Determine Your Future

I played a league match in Flushing, New York not too long ago. In between matches, I was watching two intermediate players competing. One of the players lost and simply could not understand the reason why. He came to me after the match and told me that he had beaten his opponent easily a week ago. That to me was a classic mistake of taking a past performance and equating it with a present performance. Every match is new. Every match is 50-50. Past results do not determine future results.

When Sean O'Neill beat #11 in the world, Erik Lindh, at the US Open in 1985, it probably came as quite a surprise to the Swede. Erik had beaten Sean a few weeks earlier 21-4, 21-6 in a Swedish tournament, and my guess is that he came into the second encounter with the results of the first in mind. The point here is that every match is new. If you beat a player easily in a previous match, it isn't an indication that you will win easily the next time you meet.

Also, during a tournament, it's difficult to win match after match playing your very best. It's very hard to sustain that level throughout the entire event. When most players talk about their successes, they equate their performance with amazing play. They talk about how incredible they played to win a match. This makes them feel good, thinking or knowing that they did something out of the ordinary to win the match. They believe they played better than usually expected. But this mentality ironically hinders our progress as players. We handicap ourselves by creating the false belief that we can only have great results when we are playing our very best table tennis. This is simply not true.

You are better than you think you are. Remember that past results don't dictate the future, and don't condition yourself to expect good results only when you're playing your very best! The truth is that most of the time we will not be at our best. But neither are we always playing our worst. Most of the time, we will be somewhere in between playing great and playing not so great. Good players know that it takes time to play well, so give yourself a chance to play your best.

Withstanding the Elements

We have all heard about tennis legend John McEnroe and how his anger fueled his match performance. Recently it's been said that McEnroe was putting on a show, knowing that his antics would affect his opponent and even change the momentum during key points in the match. That of course does not show good sportsmanship, but the example shows how vital a player's state of mind is to his overall performance.

A player's state of mind often determines whether their performance will be affected by external elements. Over the years, I've learned some tips and techniques to remain mentally strong in the face of external elements and not allow myself to be beaten by what I cannot control. They are:

Avoiding Judgment

If you're playing a match and you tell yourself that your opponent keeps making amazing shots, or you blame yourself for missing an easy smash; you are making a judgment. When you make a judgment, it takes you out of your game. Stay focused. Stay competing.

Using Cue Words

There can be times before or during a competition where we feel an immense amount of pressure. It's good to try using some cue words to change the atmosphere of unhealthy pressure into something more manageable. You might tell yourself "it's only a game" or "I enjoy this." Before a big competition match I usually tell myself that I like the speed, spin and art of table tennis. I tell myself that I can play well. I try and stay calm and focused.

18

Minimizing Importance

For me, the best way to deal with extreme pressure situations is to diminish their importance. It seems that in big competitions like the Olympics or the Paralympics, every single thing takes on a greater significance. Things, which might not seem important in regular competitions all of a sudden, become terribly important. The root of the problem really is the importance of these competitions themselves.

I try not to get caught up in all that kind of thinking. The only thing I know is that because of the immense scale of these big competitions, athlete performances become more volatile, making it possible for anything to happen. The immense importance that is ascribed to the Games can completely consume the athlete. The inability of an athlete to detach this heightened value from their self can be one cause of defeat. That said, I also find we can use the perception of the Game's importance to our advantage while competing.

Gaining Knowledge and Experience

Many players have trouble dealing with unusual playing surfaces, especially long pips. They often give up the moment they see a non-smooth rubber on their opponent's paddles. They may even spend the entire match blaming their missed shots on the pips. For the record, I happen to play very well against long pips! Many of my training partners think I have a special ability to play against this rubber. But that is simply not so. I just bought a racket with long pips and practiced with it so I could better understand the rubber. I used long pips on and off for six months. This helped me understand the characteristics of the rubber and made it easier to play against. Also, in my training I try and practice against many different styles. I have trained against long pips many, many times.

19

I remember a period where I was having so much trouble winning against this one player. We were going back and forth, where he would win one tournament and I would win the next. He was using this one Chinese rubber on the backhand that I hated playing against. In the end, I took the same rubber he had and used it on my backhand for a couple of weeks. Once I used the rubber, I started to understand its characteristics very well and improved playing against the rubber. My match results against this individual greatly improved.

If you have trouble against choppers, maybe it would be a good idea to become a chopper for a couple of weeks. If you try it out yourself, you could learn some things that you might not otherwise notice. Experience is a big factor for improving in table tennis. When it comes to self-improvement, there are few things that beat experience.

That said; knowledge and experience in the sport of table tennis are two different things. Although you can gain knowledge from every single match you play regardless of your opponent's level, it is important to learn from players who are better than you by watching them and competing against them. I can't say this enough: "Never be afraid to fail". Never be afraid to play against someone better than you OR weaker than you. Never be afraid to ask him or her questions, and never hesitate to study them.

I owe much of my success to many of the great players who came before me. Without them, I would have never been able to achieve the level I have been so fortunate to achieve. I also can't begin to tell you the importance of playing against players who are below your level. Competing against players who are below your level is very important to becoming a good player. These experiences are necessary to becoming a complete player.

Having a Tournament Checklist

Like I said before, things don't always go the way you want. I remember one time Team USA went to the Para Pan Am games in Costa Rica. No one told us that the tournament was played in high altitude and next to a rain forest. Needless to say, we didn't play that well.

Be prepared for anything and everything when you get to a tournament. Having a tournament checklist allows you to plan for the worst and gives you an idea of what to expect. My personal tournament checklist includes:

My primary racket, backup racket, extra rubber sheets, edge tape, sandpaper, bananas, food, snacks, balls, towel, water bottle, extra shirts, shorts, and anything else I might need.

Also, my tournament checklist includes the simple acronym *PEZ*. Imagine arriving at your big competition, experiencing a whirlwind of thoughts and emotions. Your heart is beating faster. Adrenalin is coursing through your veins. It's hard to remain focused when there is so much going on around you. But having something to remember and recite before or during the match can keep you in the right mindset, ready to battle.

The next time you're playing or preparing for a match, remember *PEZ*:

1. Placement
2. Extend the Rally
3. Zero Unforced Errors

Placement is so important in table tennis

Place the ball to your opponent's elbow if they are a shakehands player. Place the ball wide to the forehand if they play penhold. If they like to turn the backhand corner and use their forehand, play many balls down the line with your backhand to their forehand. If they like to play their backhand from the middle of the table, play one ball to their middle forehand and then to the wide backhand. Make your opponent as uncomfortable as you can.

Extend the rally

Many intermediate players try to end points quickly, resulting in unforced errors. You beat better players by being comfortable with playing longer points. Create the chance to make a winning attack. If you have a great forehand, try and set up the forehand. Sometimes attack the ball with 60% power. Be comfortable with the ball going to 10 or even 20 rallies.

World-class table tennis requires *zero unforced errors*. No free points. If the opponent wins the point, that's ok, but not if you give it away for free. Try to achieve 100% accuracy with your serve throughout an entire tournament. When you attack, use sensible shots. Many players today tend to go for power and pace, but there might be other ways to win a point. For example, proper ball placement and using a variety of different shots may be solutions too. Don't be afraid to play defensively sometimes. Give your opponent a chance to make mistakes.

Energy Management

Proper energy management is so important in tournaments. We have to use our energy wisely. I remember entering up to 8 events at the Nationals and the U.S. Open. I would be so tired halfway through the tournament. It was exhausting playing in all those events. Then a top player told me he started playing better when he would focus on 1-2 events per tournament. He preferred to focus on only one event when possible.

To control my energy levels during tournaments, I try and pay attention to my breathing. I try not to breathe too fast. I try and stay relaxed between matches. I bring energy bars and fruit in case I need it before or during my matches.

Maintaining your best energy levels depend mainly on what you do between matches and how you deal with distractions. I try my best between matches to remain neutral with regard to everything I do. I turn off my cell phone. I don't want to receive any phone calls or emails during the tournament. It may sound a little anti-social, but I want to minimize distractions. A distraction, whether good or bad, is still a distraction. Remember, anything can throw you off in a competition so you have to remain focused at all times!

Understanding Pressure

Finally, know that the pressure we feel during tournaments creates tension, and tension tells us that we need to get the match over with as soon as possible. However, the more we hurry, the worse we will probably play. The best advice I can give you when you are feeling pressure is to take a few deep breaths, and remind yourself why you are playing to begin with.

It's also good to simulate high-pressure situations in your practice and in your imagery before a match. Try and draw on what happened in the past. How did you feel at your last big competition? What were some of the distractions you had to deal with? I played in the 2004 Olympic Doubles trials with Sean O'Neill. We had won against two teams and were in a very good position to qualify for the second stage. I did not feel too much pressure because I had already qualified for the Paralympic Games and was going to Athens regardless of the result. But the next team we had to face was already out of contention. I suddenly felt our team had all the pressure because our opponents had nothing to lose. Sean told me it was just the opposite. He said the team that had nothing to lose would most likely give up at the first opportunity. We played the match and I played very conservatively, letting Sean do most of the work. We ended up winning that match.

It turned out to be a very good lesson for me because during our final match we had to face two USA National Team Members who were also out of contention. If we won the match, we would go on to face Canada to compete for the right to play in Athens. We went down 3-2 in games but came back to win 11-9 in the 7th. After that tournament, I was never worried about playing a match where my opponent had nothing to gain and I had everything to lose.

2 THE FIGHT AGAINST THE OPPONENT

An Unlikely Partnership

Table Tennis is both an individual experience and a partnership with the opponent. During practice, we focus on ourselves, improving our technical ability. But during a match, the spotlight shines on the person across the table instead. Everything we do depends on the opponent. When your opponent serves, you respond. When your opponent hits a forehand, you respond, and so on.

While you are constantly trying to push your opponent into making bad choices, often you will need to use their spin and their own speed to get the best possible outcomes for yourself. Like it or not, you need your opponent in order to reach your goal of playing to the best of your ability. Also, while it is important to impose our will on our opponents (I'll show you how to do just that in a bit), I've seen many players try to force their entire game on their opponents unnecessarily. For example, a player might have a good loop, but trying to loop the ball without a proper set up or paying attention to position will only increase the probability of unforced errors.

From now on, try seeing every match you play as an event; an event where you compete against, but also *cooperate* with your opponent. It is not just you who makes yourself great. Neither is it the opponent who makes you great. It really is a little bit of both. The sport of table tennis is a giant puzzle, a puzzle that you can only solve with your opponent's help.

Information Changes Everything

In his book *Seven Habits of Highly Effective People*, Steven Covey tells a story of how he is on a train and sees a few kids accompanied by their father. These kids are running all over the place, hanging from poles and being completely disruptive. Covey becomes increasingly frustrated with them and decides to ask the father to control his children. The father apologizes for their restlessness, telling Covey that their mother had just passed away. It's a horrible thing to hear, and it reverses Covey's thinking completely, leading him to apologize, embarrassed.

Information changes everything. Covey could have saved himself much agitation if only he knew why the children were behaving the way they did. Similarly, if we are willing to gather more information before we act, much of the frustration we experience in table tennis can be avoided.

During my matches, I always try and find out what makes my opponent uncomfortable. I want to know what gives him or her problems. I also try and find out what my opponent likes. I can then avoid playing to his or her strengths and preferences. Just like in chess, it's about placement and putting your opponent in an uncomfortable position whenever you can. Use the information given to determine how you will play the next ball.

The next time you play a match, ask yourself these questions:

- Where is my opponent standing?
- What are my opponent's tendencies?
- What does my opponent want to do?
- What does my opponent like?
- What does my opponent dislike?
- What is my opponent's mindset?
- Does my opponent fight until the end?

- Does my opponent get easily discouraged?

A problem with many intermediate players is not how much information they can process, but *where and when* they process that information. Many players I've worked with start looking at the ball only when it's crossing the net, rather than when the opponent makes contact with the ball. Many players also look at the ball leaving the opponents' racket without actually watching what the opponent is doing. Playing table tennis match without looking at your opponent is equivalent to driving a car without looking out your windshield or playing chess without looking at your opponent's pieces!

Unfortunately, this results in decisions made almost blindly. By the time the ball crosses the net precious decision-making time is lost. On the other hand, watching the ball as soon as the opponent makes contact gives us more time to process the information and make the correct shot. Focusing on our opponent essentially gives us *twice* the time to play the ball.

I remember doing multi-ball with a top Chinese coach. The aim of the drill was to play strong shots from seven different random positions – short to the forehand or middle, long cut to the backhand, two topspin balls to the backhand and then forehand from three random positions. I would win a point if I made all seven shots. The goal was to get 10 points, and honestly, I simply could not win any points at first. I was running all over the place and was totally out of balance once the drill went random. But in the end, what helped me was to focus on the coach's racket angle. I told myself not to move until I saw the angle of the racket and I could judge where the ball was going next. After that decision, I was able to keep my balance and completed the drill.

Pace, Power and Serve

When watching your opponent, it's important to note what he or she wants to do with pace and power.

Let's say the opponent is looking to use your pace against you. Make sure you don't give him or her any. For example, if my opponent likes a lot of pace on the ball, I will play much slower. Try and make your opponent as uncomfortable as possible. Never do what they want and always try and give them something they do not expect. Remember, table tennis is a sport of deception!

When I was training in Beijing, I learnt that we should use medium power for our shots, and make good use of our opponent's power and pace instead. Try hitting the ball at the top of the bounce. Our opponent's spin won't be as strong, and we can play a shorter stroke. By doing this we can be more deceptive in our direction and take time away from our opponent.

When our opponent is using 80% of their power, we should be hitting the ball using 20% of our power. These types of shots can be very powerful and are much easier to execute from a physical standpoint. This also makes sense when we want to do combinations, connecting shot after shot.

Finally, always ask yourself what the opponent wants to achieve with the serve. Does he want to get into a chopping rally? Is she looking to slow spin the ball? Is he looking to smash? Is she looking to block?

Playing the Player

Every match is different. So is every opponent you face. It is critical to adjust your tactics to the level and tendencies of your opponent.

The best way to improve is to become stable in your game. We don't always play our best, but we should try and avoid playing our worst when we can. Many players try and train so that they can have wins against the top players. What they sometimes miss is that it is just as important to be able to beat the players below you. The best way to improve is to try and move your low level up. Let's use the USATT rating system for this example. If your range of play is 400 points and you are rated 2100, that means you can have wins or losses from players who are rated from 1900-2300. What if you could eliminate the losses from the 1900-2100 players? That is what it means to bring your low level up.

Many players want to focus on playing against people who are above their level, thinking that by beating those players, they will become much better themselves. It is important to play players above you and equal to you, but also those who are below you. Many players enter rating events above their level, hoping to be able to upset a higher rated player. They fail to realize that if they beat players at their level and below, they will improve much faster. It is also easier to find ways to beat players below you than to find ways to beat players above you. If you want to improve the fastest, work on bringing the low parts of your game up. You can do this by competing against players who are slightly lower in level than you. Make your standard deviation smaller and you will improve faster and become more stable. By doing this, you will have better chances to win entire tournaments rather than just beating one or two higher rated players.

In New York City, many different clubs have weekly leagues. In some of the leagues, there are players who are intermediate and beginners. I make it a point to play those league matches whenever I can. I make sure that I take every match seriously. I work hard if a player is 600 points rated below me or 150 points rated above me. I go into the match the same exact way whether I am playing a beginner or professional. I might play the match differently, but my mindset is the same. I have to compete against this player regardless of how much better they are than me or how much worse they are than me. Table tennis is not about who is a better player, but who is better on that day.

Playing Someone Stronger

To overcome a better player is no easy task. It may sound intuitive, but the best way to achieve success over a player with greater ability than your own is *to make your own game stronger*. In other words, defeating a better player comes from your own strength.

You cannot impose the will of your game on this type of player because their ability surpasses your own. To make your own game stronger, you need to eliminate unforced errors. You need to put your opponent into risky situations. Use the factors of pressure and the importance of the match to gain an equal footing over your opponent when you are not equal to them in ability.

Against a higher-level opponent, it is important that you get him or her to play worse than usual rather than forcing yourself to match his or her level. You won't be able to do that by trying to bully them off the table, pulling out shots from outer space. So, when your opponent is better, keep it simple. Serve simple. Kong Linghui (World Table Tennis Champion and Olympic Gold Medalist) had a very simple backhand serve but it was very effective against many different players. When you are playing someone better than you, it's probably best not to overcomplicate the game for yourself.

A few years ago, I played a tournament against a top Chinese player. Normally when I play these types of players I try and end the point as soon as possible. But I was having a lot of pain in my lower back that day and I could not kill the first ball very well. I then decided to play more of a controlled game, creating chances to kill the ball rather than trying to end the point as quickly as possible.

I won the match comfortably in the end. I began to understand that the way to beat better players was not to kill every single ball, but instead to control and redirect their power. Try to place the ball better and change the position, speed and spin of the ball constantly. When

31

someone is better than us, we do not want to put ourselves into a position where we are forced to make a big shot, a stroke that will either win or lose us the point. In those positions, it will be hard to win the match. It is much better if we force this choice upon our opponents.

Playing Someone Weaker

The same concept applies to players who are lower rated than me. If someone is a beginner, I also show him or her that I am there to compete. I compete in the same way as if my opponent was a professional. That way, competing eventually becomes a habit.

I asked world-class player and US Open Champion Cheng Yinghua what level his opponents have to be in order for him to play seriously. He said if the player is rated 1600 and above, he has to try and do something to win the match. Otherwise, he might lose. This is coming from a player who was consistently rated over 2800 and at his best was probably around #16 in the world!

Another reason I started playing well was because I spotted points to players who were lower than me. I would give them up to 17 points in a 21-point game. This forced me to reduce my mistakes. I had to learn to play tight table tennis. It made me a much better player.

I had an awesome practice with a 1400 rated player at a club in Flushing, New York the other day. We played a few matches. I first gave her 7 points and won 3-1. Then I gave her 8 points and won 3-1. Then I gave her 9 points and won 3-1. But these matches were tough. I couldn't afford to give away even one free point. I noticed that I was at a disadvantage whenever I got into quick rallies. I had to do everything I could to slow down the pace of the ball. That way I could compete better.

Next time you are at your table tennis club and you see a much lower rated player, give that player some points and play a few matches. You will be surprised by how much the both of you can improve. If you can compete in every match you play, you will find that you will increase your winning percentage tremendously, regardless of your opponent's level.

Imposing Your Will

Ultimately, good players impose their will on their opponents. I think most intermediate players have a problem imposing their game on the other player. But imposing our will on our opponent does not mean we remain static and stick to a specific strategy. As a matter a fact, it means just the opposite! To impose our will on our opponent is to be changing all the time. We need to keep our opponent guessing. We need to deceive them. Table Tennis is a sport of adjustment, adaptation, and deception.

Returning to a previous example, we might have a great looping game and want to try and topspin every ball in the match no matter what. This can work against a player below or equal to our level. But a better player will always seek to impose his or her will and try to stop us from doing what we want.

In turn, if you find your opponent trying to stop you from asserting your game, do something else instead! Instead of looping every single ball, try pushing the ball back heavy close to the table or topspin the ball slowly over the table. Sure, these strokes might not be what we're most comfortable with, but sometimes we need to do what's uncomfortable rather than staying in our comfort zone and losing the point automatically. We should never force a losing game on our opponent. We should create positions where our opponents must beat us, if they can.

One quality of a successful player is being able to play table tennis when we can't do what we want. We need to be uncomfortable in our practice. Our coaches and trainers and practice partners should make things difficult for us.

Scouting Out Your Opponents

You can get knowledge from the most unlikely sources. Everyone has something to contribute. I was recently at a tournament in Europe. I spoke to someone about a Chinese player that I had to play in the next match. This person never played the Chinese player, but watched him many times. He gave me some great tactics and advice, and I ended up winning the match. The player I beat was the #1 Chinese Para Player in the world. Without this person's tactics, I might not have won the match.

It is very important to scout out your opponent and get information from multiple sources. Try and find someone who has played your opponent before. Ask them about your opponent's serves, return of service and style. Talk to people who have observed your opponent. See if you can watch your opponent playing against other players. Be careful to pay attention to what your opponent does when the match is close. What serve does he like to use? How does she construct the point? Does he play defensive or aggressive? Know your opponent and know them well.

The Distance Between Us

The game of table tennis changed from a 21-point scoring system to an 11-point scoring system a quite a few years ago. Due to the short duration of the game, every single point has now become even more important. The server also has a big advantage. Whoever misses their serve could possibly be surrendering 12-13% of the entire game.

There are also times when the value of a single point can be worth two, three and in some cases even four points. We are trying to get to 11 points, but so are our opponents. This means that we should not only be concerned with how close we are we to 11 points, but also how close we are to our opponent's score.

For example, you're trailing your opponent 5-7. A point is about to be played. If you lose that point, the score is 5-8, and the distance between you and your opponent becomes three points. But if you win, the distance between you and your opponent is just a solitary point.

Now imagine you're leading 8-5. You win the point and go ahead 9-5. You lose the point and it's only 8-6. At 9-5, you're two points away to victory. At 8-6, the distance between you and your opponent is much closer than 9-5.

At these important points during the game, it'd probably be better to go for high percentage shots rather than outright powerful winners. That way we can increase the chances of either maintaining the distance between our opponent if we're leading, or closing the distance if we're behind.

Also, some players save a special serve till the end of the game. While this is good, we shouldn't be afraid to use it early if it allows us to gain an important advantage as well.

3 THE FIGHT AGAINST THE BALL

The ball essentially defines the sport, but interestingly people don't really think about the ball as much as they think about themselves, their opponent or other match factors.

I was playing in a tournament in Slovenia not too long ago. My opponent was from Russia, and he had a very strong attack from both sides. He was serving very heavy backspin to my forehand. The serve was so heavy that I had to keep my racket low to get under the ball. However, when I moved back to my ready position to play the point, my racket was still low. My opponent then looped to my backhand, and because my racket was low, I could not get on top of the ball, conceding many points since I was unable to block his first topspin.

Sometimes we focus on a stroke we previously executed instead of the stroke we need to play at that moment. A past action could still stay in our mind as a present action. In my mind, I was very concerned with receiving the serve because my opponent had such a strong first attack. Subconsciously I was keeping my racket low, even though I knew I had to keep my racket up to make a good quality block.

This same problem might happen to you. You might have just played a loop with your backhand against a backspin ball, and then you loop the next ball off the end of the table. Your opponent blocked your first loop and the ball came back different than the chop he first gave you. What happened was that your mind was still concerned with the under-spin ball. As a result, you could not adjust to the next ball.

The solution to this problem is paying attention to the changes of the ball, thinking about what is coming next, as well as preparing properly to play the next ball. When players do not pay attention to the changes of the ball, they find they cannot keep a good rhythm with the ball. We can avoid many unnecessary mistakes by being aware of the ball's changes.

The Ball Always Wants To Do Something

One thing we realize when we play a match is that the ball never takes a fixed position. The ball is constantly changing. To be a better player, we have to understand the ball, pay attention to the ball, adjust to the ball and make it work for us.

I was at the US Open last year playing against a very strong player. He had made the USA National Men's Team previously. His loop had so much spin on it, and to make things worse, it was traveling at such a high arc because he was so tall. I decided I would try and hit the ball into the net whenever he looped. My reasoning was that if I tried to hit the ball into the net, it might go on the table because the ball had so much topspin. I ended up winning the match.

I realized something important that match - the ball is *always* trying to do something. If the ball has heavy backspin, it wants to go into the net. If it possesses heavy topspin, the ball wants to go off the table. As long as I make sure my racket doesn't go where the ball wants to, I have a good chance of getting the ball back onto the table. If the ball has backspin and my racket is moving downwards, the ball will most likely go to the net. If the ball has topspin and I counterattack with my racket moving too much forward, most of the time the ball goes off the end.

In table tennis, there are three situations where we play the ball. The first is when we don't impart any speed on the ball. This could be a chop or a stop block. The second is where 80% of the speed comes from our opponent. This could be a counter-loop off the bounce or a fast block. The third involves attacking and imparting our own speed to the ball, for example, looping against a regular block. It is good to remember these things when we play a match. We need to choose the correct response based on the type of ball directed at us, and the situation we're in.

Making the Ball Work for You

1. Create the Proper Distance

One of the most important aspects of table tennis is being able to create the proper distance between yourself and the ball. When conditions are different or when our opponents are making things difficult for us, we need to be able to create the right distance between the ball and ourselves so that we have more options, more choices and more time.

Every player has a comfortable position where they are able to play their best strokes. Players that have longer strokes tend to be comfortable attacking away from the table, and players with shorter strokes prefer to attack closer to the table. So try and play the ball deeper when your opponent is closer to the table. When they are away from the table, try and take pace off the ball or play even wider angles to force more court coverage. It is your job to constantly keep them out of their comfort zones, while at the same time creating opportunities for yourself to get into a good position and play your best and most sensible shot possible.

The key to creating the best distance between yourself and the ball is to focus on your feet. This means adjusting your body movement and position based on ample space on the forehand and letting the ball come closer to you on the backhand.

Table Tennis is a game of placement and as mentioned earlier "deception." It's a good idea to try and keep your opponent guessing by changing the location, depth, speed and spin of the ball when you can.

2. Proper Ball Contact

When we attack the ball, the energy transfer should take place right at the point of contact. Concentrate all your energy and power when contacting the ball. In order to accomplish this, we need to do a few things. Try and get as close to the ball as possible when attacking. Pass the racket through the ball. Make sure you hit the ball in the middle of your racket during a forehand shot. Contacting the ball with the top of your racket greatly diminishes its speed!

Move your hand slow when the ball travels fast. Slow down your shot if your opponent increases his or her pace. For example, you serve and the opponent pushes to your forehand. You loop the ball at a medium speed and they block the ball fast. You cannot loop at the same speed again. Slow your hand down. Use the speed of the ball. Many players make the mistake of increasing the speed of their ball, taking an unnecessary high risk. Know when you should attack the ball fast and when to attack the ball slow. Try and adjust your hand to the incoming speed and spin of the ball.

3. Develop Good Ball Control

Consistency is the first and most important step to becoming a good player. Try and master good ball control before you start using more power on your attacks or counterattacks. When I train with my students, it is important that they can push a hundred balls in a row, that they can hit a hundred forehands and backhands non-stop. Many intermediate players are inconsistent, having probably not paid much attention to practicing consistency during the beginning phase of their training. They find themselves uncomfortable with long rallies and as a result, try to end points as quickly as possible.

With the way the sport is played today, we need to be able to attack continuously. We can generate more power when we use a wider stance, and we need to stay balanced when we are attacking and defending. One of the most, if not the most important skill to being a good player is being comfortable engaging in long rallies. The only way you can do that is by being consistent.

4. Reduce Mistakes

Rather than rushing to attack the ball, we can reduce mistakes on the first shot by spinning the ball with a good arc and quality spin.

Reducing the backswing on our forehand can help us make better quality shots as well. Many players generate power on the forehand stroke by just using their arm, resulting in a long backswing. The longer the backswing, the higher the chance for error. These errors are in turn, mostly due to timing. Generate power from your weight transfer instead of just your arm. It is also important to make sure you are applying shoulder rotation when using your forehand. This will help reduce backswing as well.

5. Change the ball's trajectory

When looping against under-spin, make sure your ball is not traveling in a straight line. Try to create an arc. This is very important especially on the backhand loop. When looping an under-spin push with the backhand, it may be best if the ball travels slow and with more spin rather than with less spin and more speed.

When looping with a higher arc, it is also important to play the ball deep towards the end line. When you loop the ball deep, your opponent has to do two things: adjust their racket angle and stress their body and ball position. This will also reduce their reaction time and increases the chance for error. If you drive your first ball to a bad location, such as directly cross-court or into your opponent's racket, he or she does not have to adjust the angle. The chance for error from the player is decreased. It's also harder for you to make another offensive shot after the block. When we drive the ball, it should be well placed. We should also be careful that the player does not use our own speed ;

It's important to be aware of the ball's depth of bounce
allow the ball to bounce in the middle of the table, our opponents are able to use the speed of our ball against us, blocking close to the table. Looping the ball deep to the end-line forces your opponent to stand further away from the table, and it gives you more time because the ball itself has to travel a greater distance to reach your opponent. This also gives your opponent less angles.

Usually when a player has not learned about placement, the depth of their bounce when attacking is at the middle of the table. If the opponent were close to the table, such a shot would probably be a mistake. That being said, a slower, higher, deeper loop placed to the body of your opponent is a very good weapon when they are standing close to the table.

Remember; only use as much speed as you are prepared to deal with yourself. If you expect your opponent to get the ball back, use changes of speed, spin and placement to get a ball you can put away.

6. Improve shot quality

I gave a lesson to a new student a few weeks ago. She is on the table tennis team of a well-known college in New York City. As I was training her, I noticed that although her technique was decent, the quality of her ball just wasn't as good. I was able to return her attacks without doing too much. I thought maybe if she could increase her racket speed when she was getting close to contacting the ball, this could help her get a better-quality attack.

I had a dilemma here. This was a player who had an attack that just wasn't penetrating. If this player were unable to put more pressure on her opponent, she would not be able to improve her level very much. I thought about teaching her how to use her opponent's speed and how to play quicker, but what I really wanted was to find a way to improve her contact with the ball.

Better players have good balance, good technique, and many times during a match use minimal effort to impart good speed and spin on the ball. The fastest and easiest way to improve overall is to improve the quality of your shot.

The next time I work with that student, I will focus exclusively on improving the quality of her shot. I will do this by getting her racket to move faster when she is making contact with the ball. I will make sure she passes through the ball after she makes contact. I will work on getting her to transfer power into the ball with good weight transfer and proper position from the ball.

This reminds me of a time when I returned to New York City after playing two tournaments in Europe, I realized that the quality of my ball had improved quite a bit. In Europe I was playing against better players, and I had no choice but to modify my technique so I could compete. I made my stroke shorter. I also made sure to accelerate my racket speed as I was coming close to the ball. I also tried to use my opponents' power against them.

To improve the quality of your shots, add spin first, and then follow with speed when looping or driving the ball. This is very important. When you contact the ball, make sure you feel yourself generating spin first, and then follow the ball with speed. If you generate speed first, you will find that the ball leaves your racket too quickly, and the amount of spin you make is diminished. Also, you will find that because the ball has left your racket so quickly, your control of the ball has diminished as well.

One thing I learnt from Chinese coaches is that you need to feel your fingers when you are looping or counter-looping over the table. Most of us try and counter close to the table with our forearm. Next time, try to use your fingers and your wrist at the same time. This applies as well to receiving short serves. Focus more on using your fingers when your opponent serves short or when you are dealing with an incoming topspin loop. Almost try and feel the ball with your fingers. Try and imagine your fingers are moving into the incoming topspin loop or incoming serve.

As I mentioned, many players have a problem with the quality of their attack. I think more time should be spent on trying to improve the quality of the attack. When you attack, you should be able to impart good spin and speed on the ball.

7. Location, Location, Location.

Remember, there is always a choice when you are touching the ball. You can do so many things. Do not limit yourself. For example, if you are in a rally and you are looping, you don't have to continue looping all the time. You can fish or chop the ball if you feel you might loop yourself out of position. Remember location is important. Put the ball on the table where it makes the opponent the most uncomfortable. Put the ball to your opponent's body, and alternate between slowing down and speeding up. Change the height of your loops and so on.

Down the Line

When you flip the ball, try and flip for a good position. You don't have to flip to make an outright winner. Strategic players use a quick, deep push as a tactic when receiving serves. A good receiver does not move too early. They wait to see what is happening.

Try and go down the line more rather than just cross-court. Many players have a difficult time when we play down the line. It makes them uncomfortable. It is much easier for them to play a ball cross-court because that's what they usually practice the most.

I win many points when I use my backhand down the line to my opponent's forehand. Many players have a very strong forehand attack from their backhand corner; it is good to play your backhand out to their forehand, especially against pen hold players.

The Middle

The middle is a shakehands player's weakest point. Try and play the ball directly at your opponent's elbow when playing these types of players. Play the middle. This limits the time your opponent has to make a decision. They have to choose between using a backhand or a forehand. This process of thinking gives the opponent less time to execute the stroke.

Playing the middle also means finding our opponent's switch point. This is usually at the elbow of the opponent. In your next practice, try and play more balls to your opponent's elbow. Do this when attacking and blocking. Their elbow position is always moving because their feet are always moving. Try and use their elbow as a target for where to hit the ball.

When I was growing up and learning the game, I played many matches with a player named David Fernandez. David would later become a top player in the United States and the Central American Games Men's Singles Champion. David spent a few months in Sweden. When he returned, he started playing so many balls to the middle. David became awesome at playing any weak ball into the middle of his opponent. Because David was so good at this particular shot, I got amazing practice dealing with balls that were placed into my middle. This later became a big factor in increasing my overall playing ability.

I recommend doing drills where you have to deal with the middle ball without using footwork. Have your coach give you multi-ball randomly to the middle and see if you can return these balls just using your hand. The rule of thumb is if you are close to the table use your backhand, and if you are far from the table use your forehand.

The Second Middle

Besides the elbow, I learnt I needed to attack my opponent's hip as well. I would alternate between attacking their right and left hip. This helped me overcome opponents who blocked really well. Instead of trying to get the ball past them, I would attack their second middle. I would also sometimes attack directly to the right hip using my backhand and then very wide to my opponent's backhand using my backhand.

Specific Stroke Mechanics

In general, we should be working to make our techniques more compact, using shorter movements. We should pay close attention to weight transfer. We should also work on the development of power from the legs and hips as well as accelerating racket speed when we contact and pass though the ball. Training is more effective when done in a comprehensive and concise manner.

Moving to the Forehand

It's easy to lose position when you move to the forehand, usually because it's very hard to get the proper shoulder rotation needed to make the best attack, as opposed to a forehand shot from the backhand side. We need to make sure we don't lose our position when we move to the forehand side. We can do this by using higher a quality placement when we attack. It is also good to move using both our feet.

As was mentioned earlier, many times I try and direct my backhand to my opponent's forehand. Most of my opponents simply do not like this type of ball because they are usually looking to turn and use their forehand from their backhand side.

Forehand Smash and Loop

When you smash with the forehand, turn your shoulder back a little bit. Do not keep your elbow so close to your body. Make sure you pass through the ball and you go forward. If you are looping in a rally, sometimes try and change the height of your loops. Sometimes loop the ball high and sometimes drive the ball straight. You want your opponent to have to adjust their racket angle when they block your loop. You can do this by varying the loop. If the loop is the same all the time, your opponent only has to put his or her racket out and will not need to adjust to the ball very much.

Forehand Block

When blocking with the forehand, the stroke must be very compact. Try and use very little movement with your hand if possible. It is important to note that most higher-level players usually try and counter-loop the ball with the forehand whenever they can.

When you block, try and take pace off the ball occasionally. Mix it up. Do not have one set block. Be able to block fast, slow, or at a regular speed. Taking the pace off the ball is also very effective when your opponent is looping away from the table.

Forehand/Backhand Chop

If you are chopping with the forehand or backhand, you can let the ball drop or you can chop the ball at a higher height. Chopping straight down on the ball and passing the racket through the ball quickly is also good. It is important to note that in table tennis you need to move the racket through the ball at a quick speed during most strokes. You should accelerate the speed of the racket when your racket is close to the ball.

Chop with a more vertical motion when the ball is coming at you fast. Chop more horizontally if the ball is coming at you slowly, going underneath the ball. When someone is ripping at you, you cannot go underneath it. The ball is traveling too fast.

Controlling Spin

It is important to understand and control spin in the sport of table tennis. The ball can possess an amazing amount of spin at times, and you need to find a way to manage that spin. USA great Danny Seemiller has often said that table tennis is simply a game of spin.

When the ball has a lot of spin, try not to jab at or reach for the ball. Get your racket close to the ball, and when you make a decision - stick with it. This is especially important during serve return. Once you decide to do something, follow it through completely.

Guide to Serving

The serve is the most important stroke in table tennis. The serve is the only time you have control over the match. It's important to know that factors of the match could dictate how you serve. These include your opponent's receive habits, tendencies, and even the score line. Jim Butler once told me that he serves quickly when he is leading, but he takes his time to serve if he is trailing or if the game is close.

We want to watch our opponent's stance and position when we serve. If you see your opponent is close to the table, give them a deep serve. If they are far, serve short. Remember, you want to use the distance between them and the table to disrupt their play. Also, use the whole table and not merely crosscourt.

Before The Serve

I've seen many players hurry when they are serving, and this is quite unnecessary. Top players take a lot more time between rallies, thinking about what serve they should do, what spin, and so on. Most importantly, they think about how the ball might be returned and what they want to do with the return.

Some top players also use certain rituals before they serve the ball. They might wipe the table with their hands or bounce the ball on the floor a few times. These habits lead to increased concentration when executing the serve.

Before you serve, relax, look around, and watch your opponent. Watch his position and watch his stance. A good player stands still for a few seconds before serving, ensuring the best concentration possible.

A few years ago, I remember training with a very high-level player who did the same serve over and over again. He served with the forehand and alternated between short no spin and light under-spin. But what

51

made the serve so tough was that he took his time. He slowly got into his service position and just waited. It took him four full seconds to serve.

It was really tough to play against this serve. Although the serve was not particularly amazing, this player's execution of the serve was outstanding. He was really meticulous in the way he served. Jan Ove Waldner once said that having confidence in your own serve is the most important aspect of serving, and that's what this player did, turning an arguably poor serve into a powerful weapon.

After watching how effective this serve was, I decided to incorporate it into my own game. When serving, I get into my ready position and count to five before serving. Sometimes I would serve at three, and other times I would serve right away. With this counting system, I could count to five and make contact with the ball anywhere from one to five. This method was effective for throwing off my opponent's timing and making my opponent hesitant with the return.

It's also good to mix and match your serves with different serving positions. You could use the same serve from the middle of the table and also from the backhand. This gives the serve a different angle and effect.

During a match, find out the location on the table that your opponent doesn't like you serving from. If your opponent likes to receive with his backhand on the whole table, it might be good to serve short to the forehand leaving his wide backhand open after the receive.

You should also look at the position of your opponent. Where they are standing and what area they are trying to cover. The left-handed opponent might be standing in the middle of the table trying to cover a weak forehand. In that case, you can serve some balls down the line to your opponent's backhand.

When you play someone that you have never played before you should usually try several different service positions. The same serve from different positions will have very different effects.

During The Serve

We should contact the ball very close to the table when serving. Your paddle should be as close to the white line as possible when you make contact. This decreases the distance between the ball and our opponent's racket, giving our opponents less time to react.

Also, when serving, aim for the bounce on the opponent's side to be below net height. The serve should be flat, with a low forward trajectory. World champion and Olympic gold medalist Kong Linghui had a very simple backhand service, but it bounced very low over the net. Many world class players had a tough time making an effective return, showing that simple serves can also be effective as long as they are kept low. A low bounce forces your opponent to receive the ball by moving his paddle upwards in order to lift it by creating an arc. The ball will have less force and travel slower, giving you more time to get into the best position.

When serving short, make sure the first bounce is close to the net. If you are serving long, the first bounce should be closer to the end line. You should also pass through the ball thinly and not stop too soon after impact. Many players contact the ball too softly and slowly. If you hit your other hand when serving it should hurt a lot!

You should also practice your toss when serving just like a tennis player would do. The toss of the serve is very important, and if you have a good toss, you will be able to control your serve better when it comes to placement and imparting spin on the ball. Alternate between a low and high toss to change the dynamics of the serve and keep your opponents on their toes. But also, remember to wait and contact the ball at a very low height after the toss.

Spin

Over the years, I have heard from many top players and coaches that it may be better to have one serve with multiple spins and locations rather than many different serves.

I practice against someone who constantly serves no spin to my backhand. I have to say, that is a very tough serve to return and keep low. Try and practice a serve where you can serve no spin short. The short no spin serve can be very effective, especially when used in combination with a short heavy under-spin service. Sometimes it might be better to serve no spin than under-spin. As always, this depends on what your opponent has difficulty dealing with.

When you decide to serve backspin, you can get more spin depending on where you contact the ball. You should contact the ball closer to the side of the blade, the side closer to the floor when serving with the forehand. If you want no spin, try and contact the ball higher up, preferably in the middle of the paddle.

Many players have trouble disguising their under-spin and no-spin serves. It is important to maintain the same serve action for a wide range of serves. One of the top Chinese players told me that when you serve you should move your hand fast and contact the ball with the same motion for both under-spin and no-spin. To serve no spin, do not use the wrist. Use the wrist when you choose to serve under-spin. Also, try and keep the ball as close to your body as possible when serving.

After The Serve

When practicing serves, remember to set up for your next shot. Don't watch your serve for too long. Imagine the return you will be getting. Be prepared. When you serve topspin or no spin, expect a fast return. If you serve deep, don't stand too close to the table. Back out. The ball is not coming back short. In the same way, don't serve short and back out too far. You want to stay close to the ball. Also, while serving short is good, make sure the ball isn't too short, as it will be susceptible to an easy drop shot.

In essence, decide what kind of return you want, and if possible, try to find out how the other player will return the serve. Adjust accordingly. You can't always know, but you should always have some idea of how your opponent might return your serve and what you plan to do with the next ball. For example, if you serve from the side of the table and your opponent gives a strong return, move the next serve closer to the middle of the table to diminish the strength of his/her return.

Guide to Serve Receive

Remember that everyone has trouble returning serves, not just you! Being able to return serve takes experience and practice. In general, good receivers do not move too early. They wait and see what is happening. A short serve is not coming fast. You have time to react.

When receiving, maintain a neutral stance and position your paddle above the table. Your arm should be pointed toward the net, elbow bent, ready to go in either direction. The receive stroke also does not have to be too long. Go straight at the ball. You don't need to start the stroke off the table or at the baseline. Make *quick shorter movements* when receiving serves instead of long, slower ones.

Left-handed players may receive more with their backhand over the table to better deal with sidespin from a pendulum serve. Traditional penholders should mostly receive with their forehands. When flipping a serve, it's a good idea to add topspin and create an arc. Flip at the top of the bounce. It's the biggest "window" to make your shot. Flip for position and rarely flip for winners.

Also, remember to figure out what your opponent wants to do with the serve. If you can't read the spin, you have to assume something. Be decisive. Indecision is one of the worst to things to do when receiving serves.

If the player moves their racket in one direction, try and move your racket in the opposite direction to counter the spin. When the ball is moving slowly, it usually possesses very heavy under-spin. It is difficult to make an under-spin serve move fast. Try and watch where your opponent contacts the ball when they are serving.

Receiving Short Serves

Many people I play against, including some of my students, don't understand how to move in properly to return a short serve. I learnt from my coaches that on most short serves you should step in with your primary foot and then back out.

When the serve is very short or far away, move the left foot first before the right (right before left for left-handed players.) To back out away from the table, do the opposite.

You should get close to the ball when dealing with short serves. You should lead with your elbow so your forearm is more parallel to the net. This gives you the option of going in either direction with the shot. If your head is close to the racket when you are receiving a short serve you will be able to have a quality follow through with balance.

Squeeze your forefinger and your thumb when you return a short serve with the forehand. By doing this you are automatically tightening your wrist. This allows for super fine motor control. The rest of your fingers and hand should be relaxed.

When doing short receive practice, break it up into 5-minute blocks to keep it from getting too boring. Always move out after a short receive, do not linger over the table.

Receiving Long Serves

When receiving a long serve, don't rush. Instead, keep your neutral stance, and contact the ball at the top of the bounce. You should keep a neutral stance when you are returning serve. This is very important for me because I personally tend to rush a bit when someone serves long. Remember, the rule of thumb is to contact the ball at the top of the bounce. If you can do this, your serve return should become more consistent.

When I am in trouble and I have no idea how to return a particular long serve, I move off the table and chop the ball. I started doing this because I noticed that choppers usually do not miss many serves.

Finally, don't try and kill the ball. Spin it on the table. If you dor spin the first ball, try and attack the ball with 60% of your power to good location. One component of a good receive is to spin half-loi serves. Pushing them gives the opponent too much time. Use a sho swing when you are attacking long serves close to the table.

Choosing the Right Equipment

It's important to choose right table tennis equipment for your style. Looping the ball with a thinner rubber produces more spin, but because the speed is slower, the opponent has more time to react, making it easier for them to return the ball back. When the ball is faster, the spin imparted to the ball is less, but there's also less time for the opponent to react. As a result, the opponent has more trouble dealing with spin with speed added. That said, a good player could and will use a combination of speed and spin together when attacking.

I found that using a rubber with a 2.1mm thickness allows me to get the best combination between speed, spin and control. Every player has his or her own comfort level when it comes to equipment. They try different things and find what works for them. However, it is important to see what equipment good players use. This can give you some ideas as to what could work well for your own game too.

4 THE FIGHT AGAINST OURSELVES

The One Match That Changed Everything

I feel I became a high-level table tennis player because of one mat
and what it did for my self-belief. Without this match, I do not believe
would have reached the top level.

The year was 1998 and I was in the final of a very big competition
New York City against a top USA player. I could not compete w
because I did not believe in my own abilities and myself as a player. B
my coach at the time told me I was going to win the tournament. F
believed in me even when I did not. My opponent was up 16-14 in tl
fifth but I ended up winning 21-19.

Everything changed for me once I won that tournament. Somethir
in my mind switched on. I always had a desire to beat everyone that
went up against. But after that match, I truly believed I could wi
Whenever I enter the competition hall, I feel I am able to compet
Before that tournament, I felt as though I was invisible when I walkr
into a competition hall. I was a pretender who just showed up. But no
I was a competitor, and while I still had much to learn, I knew I cou
compete with anyone. It was just a matter of time…

Confidence and Self-Belief

Former world champion Jan Ove Waldner once said that the single most important factor to serving well in a tournament match was confidence. When I was at the Olympic Training Center, I was told that there was never an athlete who won who did not believe they could win. Self-confidence is the belief in your own ability to succeed. For me, the projection of self-confidence is very important. I want to feel confident, and I want my opponent to see that, both during and after a match.

As we mentioned, a table tennis tournament is a platform for us to compete. That is all there is to it. Nothing less, nothing more. When I walk into any competition venue, I walk with confidence. I don't walk around thinking I will win every match. I don't walk around thinking I will lose. I walk around thinking I can compete with anyone at the tournament. And I know I can. This does not mean I will win all the time, but winning is not the point. The tournament is about competing, period. If there is anything else going on in your head, then your ability to compete will be affected.

Most good athletes have a high level of self-confidence and more importantly, the ability to maintain that level of self-confidence over time. While having self-confidence does not mean we do not have negative thoughts; good athletes believe in their ability to perform regardless of the obstacles they face.

The most important success to any endeavor is self-belief. There is hardly ever a champion who did not believe in their own self and abilities. When I look at the players I have to compete against, I try not to think about how good they are, or what great results they might have had. Each new match is an individual event. It doesn't matter if I have beaten someone a hundred times in the past or lost a hundred times to the person before. When I walk onto the table for a new match, history is irrelevant. Believe in yourself. You can do it. Each match is a new event.

61

Every new event is a fresh start. It's a blank page.

When you get on the table, you must believe that you can do it. Ha\
faith in your abilities no matter how sub-par or great they are. Get on tl
table with confidence. Know in your heart and mind that you ca
compete. Never be afraid of failure and never try and impress others wi
your performance. Do not define your self-image by a faile
performance. Separate the two so that you and your coach can analy:
your matches properly. When you believe you can compete you s
yourself up for a great battle between you and your opponent. That
when you truly get the chance to enjoy the real nature of competition.

Don't Build Yourself Walls to Climb

I was in graduate school full-time and was scheduled to play one tournament in Romania and another in Spain. USA Table Tennis, for funding reasons, decided to send me to a tournament in Slovakia and one in Slovenia six weeks earlier than the ones in Romania and Spain.

I called up Stellan Bengtsson and told him I would play the tournaments in Slovenia and Slovakia, but I didn't think I would be ready. I started to explain my training and told him I needed time to prepare to play my best. Stellan told me that I shouldn't build myself walls to climb. My opponents would already be trying to tear me down, so why make their job any easier?

It is important to stay positive when we go into our matches. We should not use any phrases that will tear us down, nor entertain any negative thoughts or ideas. In other words, if I say to myself "I won't be playing at my best this tournament" or "my opponent won the nationals twice, he is so much better than me", I set myself up for failure. Your opponent is trying to tear you down, so why help them? Do the opposite. Always stay positive, and always play with confidence.

The following are some common negative thoughts or assumptions that we need to remove from our vocabulary:

1. *"I have to play a specific way all the time."*

No, you don't have to loop every single ball. You don't have to rip the ball with your forehand all the time. Develop other parts of your game. Try not to play a game that is too one-dimensional. Try and vary what you can do. Remember, in the match the focus is on your opponent, not you! If you have a great forehand, try and develop other parts of your game so you can increase the opportunities for your forehand to get into play.

2. *"Results define who I am."*

Many players have a problem of equating self-worth with table tenn
results. It is normal to feel great when you win a tournament or a goo
match, and it is normal to feel not so great when you lose. But if I a
generating intense feelings based solely on my results, then something
wrong.

Avoid defining who you are by your results. Instead, focus more c
fighting, on competing. The act of succeeding in table tennis is staying
the present moment, competing to the best of your ability. It is tho:
who can find enjoyment in battling their opponent that will become tl
most successful.

3. *"I hate it when the games are close."*

Many of us feel uncomfortable when we are playing a match and tl
score is close. The score is 9-9 in the fifth. Our hands are shaking, ar
we absolutely can't wait for the match to be over. The thing is, v
shouldn't feel so much stress when the games are close! Neither shou
we be focused on the match outcome rather than the match itself. Durii
the match, we need to focus on tactics and competing, rather than wh
will happen if we win or lose the match. Once our thinking in a match
affected by the future, we are unable to perform to the best of our abilit
and we actually remove ourselves mentally from the match!

4. *"I can compete, but not defeat..."*

A top American player once said he thought there were some playe
who could compete, but never win. Or in his words, they can "compe
but not defeat." I believe this player was not correct in his assessmer
When we compete properly, we always have a chance to win. Winnir

64

never comes before competing. Competing is always first. Again, we cannot control our match results, but we can choose how we compete. Control what is controllable. Let everything else take its own natural course.

One thing that made Waldner so great was that you could not tell by his expression whether he had just won or lost a match. There are times when I feel as though I cannot compete against my opponent, but I never let my opponent see that. Even if my opponent is a world-class player, I show up to the table as if we are equals. I want them to know that I am there to compete. I watch matches where intermediate players play against top players, and the intermediate player is laughing and having a good time, making no attempt to compete. I remember beating a particular player rated 300 points below me. After the match the player came up to me and said he saw how good I was and felt as though he had no chance to win. He said he did not even try and thought he could have played better. Classic mistake! This player could have given me a good match, but I won the match doing nothing. In table tennis, we should be competitive-minded no matter how good our opponent is.

5. "I can't seem to close out the match."

I've had many students speak to me about leading but being unable to finish or close out the match. I am asked many times if there is anything they can do to find a way to solve this problem.

The reality is that table tennis *can be* stressful, and it's ok to feel a bit of stress before a match. But what can be problematic is when we take that stress into a match by thinking about the outcome once we go up 10-6 in the final set or are leading 2-0 in games.

The mind cannot do two things at once. If all we are seeing is the outcome of the match, we cannot perform to the best of our abilities at the same time. Once we are in a match and we are thinking about winning or losing, we are in some serious trouble. I remember I was in the sem final of the 2006 IPC World Championships. I was up 7-4 in the fin game against a world-class player. I then started thinking about the resu and the match was over. I couldn't believe it. I lost 11-8 in about on minute.

What happened was that I started to feel pressure once I focused c the result. I stopped doing what I did to get me to the point of being u 7-4 in the final game. All I wanted to do was win the match. I starte trying to finish all the points as quickly as possible. I went complete outside my game. I stopped competing. I also let the pressure contr me. The amount of pressure was so high once I saw the win was possibl

Now I try my best to focus on competing regardless of the score. know that the match is not finished until the opponent and I shal hands. Are you up 10-6 in the fifth game? Try telling yourself you a down 10-6. This takes the can pressure off you and can move you mo towards the controllable present instead of the uncontrollable future.

6. "I have to play my 'A' game to win."

Two players of equal caliber are often able to shut down each other best game, or "A" games. More often than not, a player is forced to us a "B" or even "C" game to turn the tide in his or her favor. For exampl if we're playing a chopper who realizes we are very good against cho he or she might decide to attack. The attack would be our opponent's game. This could give us more trouble than if they just chopped.

I've played against very good players whom I just cannot compe with if I insist on matching my "A" game against theirs. Instead I hav to move to my "B" game, and force my opponent to adjust. For exampl I was down 0-2 in a recent tournament and trailing in the third set. I w attacking the whole time, but I simply could not pass my opponent block. My opponent would block and counterattack most of my shot

66

putting me in trouble. I then decided to play my "C Game." I became a defensive player and moved off the table, chopping everything. I won the next three games.

Not too long ago, I was playing against a very good blocker. He also had a strong forehand counter-loop. However, I saw that he did not like it when I pushed heavy under-spin. He had so much trouble playing against this ball. So, I started many of my points like that and it made him very uncomfortable.

There is never one way to play a match. We should keep trying new things so that we can somehow find a good strategy to win. If you play someone frequently and find that you are not able to win matches, try and change the way you play. Try something different.

Channeling the Right Mental State

For some players, fear or nervousness affects the way they play. B
for me, one problem is getting angry during the match. Sometimes
works but many times it does not work. Sometimes I get so angry durii
a match it disturbs my opponent. Other times I go into a match with
clear idea of the outcome. I believe in advance that a certain result shou
occur. Ironically, I play my best when I don't think like that. Our resul
suffer when we are unable to control and channel the right mental stat

We need to be aware of the things we can control and the things v
can't. We also need to find the best way to approach the things with
our control. When we lose our mental focus by getting angry at thin;
outside our control, we lose vital energy and our results suffer. We c:
improve overall by:

1. *Having an open mind*

It's important to have an open mind during the match and mal
adjustments as you play. Being able to adapt to changes in match play
paramount. The best players do not often repeat the same mistakes.

We need to be able to adapt to the changing ball. We need to have
technique that is not static. In essence, we need to figure out where v
are getting hurt in the match and how. These are decisions and choic
we have to make almost instantaneously. We get better at making the:
choices by being aware, through practice, as well as experience.

2. *Paying attention to concentration levels*

Pay attention to your concentration during the match. Make sure yc
have full concentration at all times. Don't let your mind wander and p:
no attention to distractions. Each player has a different playii

personality. Some players are more vocal than others. Some players move around more than others. But regardless of your opponent, make sure that whatever you are doing helps enhance your concentration. Concentration can be a huge determining factor in the result of a match.

One of the most important skills in table tennis is not just to have concentration, but also to have "sustained concentration" throughout the entire match. We need to be able to focus on the task at hand from start to finish. You don't think about the past or future, you stay in the present. The present is where you have the most power.

Think back to when you were taking a math test in school, the most important test at the end of the school year. You had to be 100% focused on the test from start to finish. It should be the same during a tournament table tennis match. You should have the same mindset as if you were taking a math final. The best way to do this is to improve your focus and concentration during your practice matches. You can improve your concentration during your practice matches by staying focused on each and every point.

3. *Anticipating your opponent*

Anticipation is using information to try and figure out your opponent's tendencies. In other words, anticipation is being able to strongly guess what your opponent is going to do next. It may be important to note that around eighty percent of balls are likely to be returned to the same area from where they were attacked. Just like in chess, we can adapt and do what we like when we have an idea of what our opponent will do next.

Most players have patterns. For example, if we push the ball deep to the middle our opponent might only loop the ball and never smash. Thus, every time you make a deep push, you can automatically get ready to counter-loop or make a strong block. Many times, our opponent will have a fixed way of responding to the ball.

4. Focusing on one task at a time.

Again, the mind has trouble doing two things at once. You lo:
something in each task if you divide your attention unnecessarily.

When returning serve, focus only on the return of serve. Do not thir
about what your opponent will do with the ball once you return it. Foc
all your mental effort and concentration on returning the serve. Th
does not mean you should not watch your opponent. The only thing th
is important for that moment is making a good quality receive. Do n
allow any thought of the future to enter your mind. Focus all yo
attention on returning the serve.

I try and remember this when I play matches. I found a lot of tim
that it was not really the serve that I had trouble with, but the next b;
they were giving me. My attention was divided between the ball and wh
my opponent would do. But once I stopped focusing on what n
opponent would do with the next ball, and on the quality of my recei\
instead, I started to play better. I had more confidence. I could fully dire
my attention to the ball. Also, when I committed to a decision who
returning serve, I stayed with that decision and was more positive on n
return.

Know What You Do Well

To play your best, it's important to know what you do well, how you can incorporate your strengths into your game. For example, my game goes up when I play with heavy spin, stay close to the table and attack, and when I push serves deep with under-spin. On the other hand, my game goes down when I try to flip-kill serves and rush a point. What do you do well, and how do you implement it in your game?

We also need to know why we are winning or losing points. There are many situations where we must learn to teach ourselves. We have to know where we are strong and where we are weak. We also have to know where our opponents are strong and where they are weak. We must know what the problem is so we can take the right course of action. What is your opponent doing that is hurting you? Is it something you can adjust to in the match? Or is it a skill you need to practice?

When you are not sure what to do in a match, remember what you do well. Don't be daunted by the occasion, but rather think about the placement of the ball, try and extend the rally to create the chance to play the ball you want and give your opponent no free points. You should always be thinking about your opponent's weaknesses and how to exploit them. Good players are able to shut their opponents down and not allow them to fully play their game. Remember, you don't have to play great if you are playing smart. And the converse is true. If you are not playing smart, it does not matter how great you can play. A table tennis match is incredibly volatile. The result is never certain until you and your opponent shake hands.

The Fighter's Guide to Mental Resilience

My biggest problem in table tennis for many years was going into match with a mentality of how I thought things should be, rather tha the way things are. I used to look at a player's rating and say: "there is r way I should lose to this person." I would see someone play a match ar tell myself that this person has no chance to beat me. I would also do tl same thing if I saw someone play great, and assume I had no chance beat that person. That is a very poor way to approach the sport.

On the other hand, I had my best international wins when I realiz that the match was 50-50. I realized that I had to compete to have tl best chance of winning and anything less would not cut it. Most of tl Para players that I play against are masters of the mental game. The on way to compete with them was to increase my mental strength.

Improving your mental game helps your ability to stay in contr under pressure and increases the consistency of your performances. tend to do a lot better mentally on the international level when I am ab to manage distractions. One good thing about international tournamen is that I have to keep my mental game in check and not do too mar crazy things otherwise I will get myself ejected from the tournament. B if I can do it, then anyone can!

Although the mental game is the most important part of the sport the highest level, it is no substitute for physical or technical training. table tennis, no matter how great your mental game is, it will be all f nothing if you don't pay attention to the other areas of the sport as we

Keep Yourself in the Present

I've learned quite a few things over the past 15 years working wit sports psychologists. A few years ago, I was working with one spor psychologist at the Paralympic Games. I was given a picture of Charl

Brown and was told to write some things that kept me in the present moment. The following is what I take with me whenever I compete at an important tournament:

1. I first remember why I play table tennis. I play because I love the sport. I then focus on one word that will keep me in the present moment, a positive word. I might use the word "present" or "now." When I use this word no thoughts of the future or the past come into my mind.

2. When I feel things are not going good for me, I count to 4. I then pause, exhale, and restart. Thinking about winning and losing is low-level thinking. I replace winning with "focus" and losing with "concentration."

Speak Positively

Performance is not a random event. It is not like rolling dice or playing roulette. Performance is related to your thoughts, what you say to yourself, and what you expect of yourself. You should try and make sure the things you tell yourself are positive and are directed towards improving your performance. Also, remember that who you spend time with can affect your performance. Try and surround yourself with positive people.

Many athletes are unaware that negative self-talk can greatly harm their performance. Some players tell me that they hate competing in humid conditions. When I was in Athens at the 2004 Paralympics, there was a slight air current coming from the ceiling. A few of the athletes convinced themselves they could not compete because of the air. They created an excuse for themselves and rationalized that if they lost it would be the fault of the air current, not themselves. They lost their matches before they even started competing.

Be aware of what you say to yourself before, during, and after your competition, increasing your self-awareness. It is also important to

identify situations where you might talk down to yourself unnecessaril
Will it happen in the beginning of a competition? Will it happen if yc
are trailing in a match? Remember, anything you do in a match that
not directly related to competing in the present moment can become
strong liability to your performance. Replace negative self-talk wi
positive self-talk.

Use Daily Affirmations

One day my wife woke up to find index cards posted all over tl
house. There were cards in the garage, our bathroom mirror, and eve
on the front door.

These index cards contained what many like to call "dai
affirmations." Daily affirmations can be very helpful. I think about beii
a complete player. I try and make a list of the characteristics I need
become a complete player. For me, they represent where I am now ar
where I want to be. I would write them down and hang them all over n
house, 21 days at a time. If I went to get something out of the fridge,
would read the daily affirmation that was posted on the fridge. If I we
to do laundry, I would read the one on the laundry machine. The
affirmations helped increase my self-belief.

The following are some of my daily affirmations:
1. The tougher the match, the smarter I play.
2. I have the best backhand loop in the country.
3. I have the most consistent forehand in the country.
4. My serve and serve return are of the highest level.
5. I always have three different locations I can attack to.
6. I enjoy long rallies.
7. I play the match regardless of the score.

When I am preparing for a tournament, I write down other things, such as "I am a Paralympic Gold Medalist". One set of affirmations would pertain to improving specific skills, and another would be to convince myself that I was the tournament champion even before I played a single point.

Also, if you could give your future self a little pep talk, what would you say? Before your next tournament, write a letter to yourself. What helps motivate you? What do you want to focus on during your big competition? How can you maintain that focus? How do you want to look and feel during the competition? How can you overcome challenges that you will face during the competition? How can you remind yourself to keep focused? Write a letter to yourself outlining that message. Save it and read it at the beginning of your next big competition.

Set Goals and Visualize

When I was staying at the Olympic Training Center I learned that goal setting was just as important as having a coach. When you write down your goals, you make them visible and permanent.

I also use mental imagery all the time in big competitions to see and feel myself achieving goals. If I am feeling pressure during a big match, I don't move my feet and start to hate playing long points. I want to end the point as soon as I can because of the pressure. Hence before a big match I imagine myself enjoying the match, moving my feet for every ball and visualizing myself playing long rallies. This type of imagery has been very helpful for me.

This year I was playing a Para tournament in Slovenia where I finished with a bronze medal in the singles competition. But I started to get angry during the doubles of the team event. I was getting so frustrated and lost total focus.

I knew that if I continued to get angry, I would not be able to compete. The first step for me was to realize that the way I was feelii during the match was counterproductive. Furthermore, I was acting the match based on the way I was feeling. One of the worst things yc can do for yourself during the match is show your opponent that yc feel frustrated. So I decided right away that I had to change complete how I approached the match and also how I competed. I spoke with n coach and I did some mental visualizations. I changed my entire outloo As a result, I was able to compete the next week at the next Pa tournament in Slovakia, winning a gold medal in the singles event.

Goals are updated and replaced instantaneously. I am current training for the 2014 IPC World Championships, 2015 IPC Para Pan A Games, and the 2016 Olympic Trials and Paralympic Games. Take tin to set your goals. What are you trying to accomplish in table tenni Where do you see yourself in six months, a year or five years? Identi anything that might hinder you from achieving your goals, and addre them accordingly.

How to Evaluate Your Performance – Five Deciding Game Factors

It's easy to get caught up in who won or who lost and deduce a conclusion based solely on those results. If the end result of the match was positive, you might conclude that you played great; if the end result of the match went your opponent's way, you might be inclined to think you played poorly.

This is a mistake made by many players, and it can drastically hinder individual progress towards becoming a complete player. The complete player knows there are many different factors that add to or negate a performance.

The five most important factors in evaluating one's performance are: *physical fitness, tactical fitness, mental fitness, technical fitness* and *execution*. With these factors in mind, you can judge your performance effectively and efficiently. Taking these five factors into consideration will help eliminate generalizations from your game.

Physical Fitness

Every player has their own level of physical fitness at which they feel comfortable. After the match, one needs to determine if they were comfortable with the tempo of play and if they had the speed and stamina to keep up with their opponent. The higher the level of an opponent, the greater the demands for fitness. Footwork and consistency are the core of physical fitness. If we want to move up a level or two, we should focus on these elements during training sessions and match play. Ask yourself these questions: Were you moving quickly to the ball? Could you hang in the long points in the end? Did you feel worn out by the end of the match?

Tactical Fitness

Making smart decisions is the key to winning tough matche especially in endgame situations. Having the right plan and making tl right choices are crucial. Some players keep a journal of their opponent tendencies and habits. Other players watch videos of their opponents gain visual clues. These are the players who excel and becon extraordinary during ordinary circumstances. These players are able turn defeat into success. To accurately judge your tactical fitness, t asking yourself the following: Did I come into the match with my ov game plan or a game plan from the help of a knowledgeable coach? W I making smart decisions throughout the match? Did I avoid giving aw: free points? Did I play my strengths into my opponent's weaknesses?

Mental Fitness

Mental fitness is probably the most important part of a table tenn match. At the highest levels, mental strength is the only thing th separates two players. Some players are mentally strong, always fightir to the end. They work for every point even when their back is against tl wall. They are mentally focused on the task at hand and do not fall pr(to distractions. Consider this: Did you hustle for every point and try return all nets and edges? Were you able to stay calm and collected durir the match? Were you able to fight your opponent rather than yoursel Did you always stay positive during the match? Did you concentrate (the match itself or did you start dwelling on the outcome?

Technical Fitness

Top players spend hours and hours trying to improve their technic ability. They are innovative with their game play and constantly work (

78

correcting technical deficiencies. You should ask yourself; did the strokes you attempted make sense? Was your backswing correct? Did you contact the ball properly? What about the follow through? Did you miss any of your own serves? Did you have problems with your opponent's serves? Were you balanced when transitioning between shots? Lastly, did you try to hit with more than 70-80 percent of your total power on any shots? (Maximum power on each attack should be 75-80 percent unless you are attacking to an open court to finish a point; in that case, you can attack a bit stronger).

Execution

Execution is paramount to doing well in a tournament. Being able to execute during a match shows the quality of your tournament preparation and how you actually played the ball. Far too many players make the mistake of having correct tactics but poor execution. If this is something you've observed in your game, then more time needs to be spent drilling in practice. A great player can execute a specific set of instructions almost perfectly. If they are told to play a certain pattern or sequence, they can do so regardless of the score or any other match factors. If you wanted to serve short at a certain point in the match, were you able to serve short without the ball going long? This is execution. During the match were you able to do what you set out to do? Could you execute? Good execution helps build great experience.

Table tennis is so volatile that it often requires an amazing amount of diligent planning to produce consistent patterns during game play. You will often find that better players will take you right out of your game. Things you have been training so hard to implement in your game might only occur five or six times in an entire match. During the other points you will most likely be playing your B game, and sometimes even your C and D game. It is only when you break the game down into more

79

manageable parts that you can assess and fine-tune specific portions
your game – taking you to the next level.

Train Like You Play, Play Like You Train

I think many players train a certain way but play their match
differently. For example, I have seen some players do drills close to tl
table, yet during their matches they play almost no points close to tl
table. It is important to use the same style in your training and yo
matches. You should have an idea of how you want to play in match
and train accordingly. Not only that but, sometimes you have to adju
your game to be the most effective against your opponent.

I remember when ITTF changed the size of the table tennis ball fro
38mm to 40mm. That was quite some time ago but that was one aspe
of the game, which I had a difficult time adjusting to. It was very diffict
for my opponent to counter my backhand opening with the 38mm ba
but with the bigger ball many of my opponents were able
counterattack with a powerful forehand loop. My best shot in some wa
had become a liability.

I tried everything to make my backhand opening more powerful bt
in most cases, I was not able to make a strong opening. Even when I d
my opponent used my pace against me. Next, I tried to figure out ho
to counterattack my opponent's loop. I was concerned because I start
with a backhand loop and then lost the offense because my oppone
was attacking my first ball. I was opening with the backhand because
wanted to attack the second and third ball. But when my oppone
attacked my opening, I was unable to counter my opponent's fast attac
Since I was unable to change anything about myself and since I could n
counter my opponent's attack, I decided to focus on my opponent rath
than myself.

I noticed that when most of my opponent's hit the ball against n backhand opening, they hit the ball very hard. I also noticed that most of them did not have the best balance after they made that counterattack. (I also tried to play like my opponents so that I could get an idea of what it was like to counter-loop a strong opening). So, I changed my plan. I decided to block my opponent's counter attack instead. With my block, I could get the position back and take control of the point.

By practicing a seemingly passive shot, I managed to fix a hole in my game that my opponents were exploiting. Similarly, you too can incorporate simulated competitions into your training. Like I said earlier, I find it a good idea to look at the different aspects in table tennis as pieces to a giant puzzle. Sometimes it can be advantageous to devote an extreme amount of time to one piece. For example, we might have a specific technique or combination we are trying to perfect. It can sometimes be good to isolate the things we want to work on and practice them exclusively.

Take a skill you have been practicing and turn that skill into a match. This way, you will be able to use the skills learnt in training and directly transfer them to your own game. For example, it's a good idea to play backhand-to-backhand matches sometimes, block versus attack matches, or even pushing games.

When I was 16 years old, I used to play all these different matches with members of the Boys Club. We would have counter-looping games. We would have games where one person blocked and one person looped. We would have games where one player chopped only. If I was chopping and my opponent was looping, my opponent would spot me 10 points in a game of 21. This type of practice helped me become a more complete player.

Advice from Champions

I've talked to and interacted with many champions of our sport. Th
following are some words of wisdom I've picked up from them over th
years.

Thomas Keinath

"Most players usually look at their racket when they loop wi
the forehand. This diminishes your anticipation and makes you late fo
the next ball. We sometimes have a tendency to look at our racket whe
we loop. This causes us to lose time. You can move your eyes for a qui
second to look at your racket but do not move your head."

Atanda Musa

"We need to use our legs when attacking and sometimes we have
create time for ourselves. We can do this by looping the ball with slo
heavy spin. Most players in the USA try to rip the first ball, but we cann
rip the first ball all the time. We have to loop the ball. Your opponent
trying to take away your time. Have patience. When they loop strong yo
cannot move the racket forward. Only when the ball is of normal spee
can you get the opponent out of position and then try to counterattack

Mikael Appelgren

"On the first loop against a half-long serve your arm should not sta
out too low. You should start closer to the ball. Watch the spin. G
forward more when the ball has no spin. When you are out of positio
you should always spin the ball to get back into position and continu
the point. Many players try and hit the ball hard when they are out o

position and never really learn how to fight their way back into the point. Block closer to the table and take the ball early."

Werner Schlager

"When a player is feeling pressure, they might try and win points with their weaknesses. Know what your weaknesses and strengths are. Many people do not practice the push. The push is used in 80% of the rallies. The push really is very important and something that is under practiced and not used very much in a match. A good long heavy fast push can cause mistakes from your opponents."

Peter Karlsson

"When I was young I set my goals too big and because of that I put myself under so much pressure. You really have to like your goals. It must be something you really want to do, otherwise success will be very unlikely".

"It's only table tennis. There are things in life which are much more important than table tennis. Although I do want to win all my matches, I try to keep things in perspective".

"Everything starts in practice. What you do in the practice is what you will do in the game. The match is a mirror of practice".

"What made me into a champion was stubbornness. I have never been afraid to work hard".

Sean O'Neill

"Never worry about results and never try to satisfy others with your performance".

"It is important to balance upsets with normal outcomes and not confuse the two. Great players are capable of upsets. They raise the level and reduce their errors. They play at the upper end of their lev when it matters most. The great thing about the sport of table tennis that level doesn't guarantee a win or a loss. Forcing people to play yo game is a sign of a smart or clever player."

"If you take two players and you ask them both about the same matc many times you feel as if they are both talking about two differe matches. If I play a match with you in table tennis and after the matc we are both asked about what happened during the match. Chances a we will have two very different opinions."

"When we play a slow ball we should watch the opponent careful but when we play a fastball we should quickly get ready for the next sh regardless of what happens."

Tahl Leibovitz

The following tips were also given to me to help me improve n game. These are notes that I've taken with me to tournamen throughout my career and I believe they will serve as good reminders you as well before you play any match.

- *Keep the opponent off balance with placement and serve return.*
- *Change service and service return to keep the opponent guessing.*
- *Use shorter strokes when I am up at the table.*
- *After I loop three balls, if they counter-loop, I can win the point with block.*
- *Don't try to cream the second ball.*
- *Stay up at the table and try to play more off the bounce, but don't play the bounce so fast.*
- *Service is the first touch, attack is the second touch, and attack again is third touch. With the fourth and sixth touch, I can play stronger.*

84

- *I can only kill the ball when I have the chance or when I have created the chance.*
- *When the ball travels fast I have to move my hand slow. Also in the rally when the speed increases I have to decrease my speed. When I smash, I should try and smash at a medium pace. My first goal is to get the ball on the table.*
- *If I can control my opponent's power I could be in a good position during the match. We control the power of our opponents with good placement and off speed shots.*
- *Touch the ball at least two times before trying to win the point, unless I am presented with a good opportunity. The better the player, the more I will have to touch the ball before I can win the point with a strong attack.*
- *Play opponents as though I am playing a chopper. Be patient and choose your shots wisely.*

Epilogue: Fight for the Love of the Game

"It is not the critic who counts; not the man who points out how the stron
man stumbles, or where the doer of deeds could have done them better. T]
credit belongs to the man who is actually in the arena, whose face is marred l
dust and sweat and blood; who strives valiantly; who errs, who comes shc
again and again, because there is no effort without error and shortcoming; b
who does actually strive to do the deeds; who knows great enthusiasms, tl
great devotions; who spends himself in a worthy cause; who at the best knov
in the end the triumph of high achievement, and who at the worst, if he fails,
least fails while daring greatly, so that his place shall never be with those co
and timid souls who neither know victory nor defeat."

Theodore Roosev(

Not too long ago I was having dinner with USA National Para Team coach Angie Bengtsson in Slovakia. We were discussing a problem we had to overcome, something to do with improving team unity I believe.

Suddenly, Angie said the following: "This is nothing. My sister-in law has cancer. When I get back home, I will be with her while she does chemotherapy."

I was speechless. I could only imagine how difficult that must be for the entire family. I remember when my mother passed away from cancer and how tough it was on everyone.

Anyone that has been around Angie knows that when she was a professional player, it did not matter what was going on in her life. As soon as she entered the playing hall, there'd be nothing on her mind except table tennis. And while I too had some obstacles in my journey to becoming a top table tennis player. I don't think I was able to keep my focus as well as Angie did.

Angie's words, "this is nothing" impacted me. The problems in table tennis were nothing for Angie because she had bigger and more important issues to face.

Things in our lives can affect our ability to think and play our best table tennis. It is important to know what is going on in your life. Distractions may include overtraining, personal or family problems, high expectations, low self-confidence, or seeing our results as more important than enjoying the game. I remember I was in the final of a Para Open event and up 2-0 in games. All of a sudden, I started thinking about college and what I was going to do after I graduate and how I would pay my tuition. I lost that match rather quickly.

Because of the external distractions in my life, I have had to work harder to get into the right frame of mind when I compete. It's not something that happens for me instantly. It's a process that takes days, weeks, and sometimes even months. I have been playing table tennis for more than 20 years since my first international tournament at the US

Open in 1993, and table tennis has become a form of therapy for me. A the 2014 Slovakia Open, I had the best mental performance of my li during the class 9 singles event. We can always keep improving no matt how long we've been playing or how old we are.

I watched two players in particular over the last few years. Both a great individuals, and they have gone from being rated 1200 to arour 1650. But they take the game so seriously and have zero enjoyment the sport. They believe that it makes a huge difference to be rated 160 or 1900, or whatever.

But in many ways, it is meaningless. The most important part playing this sport is to love what you are doing. Michael Jordan has clause in his contract called *"for the love of the game."* This meant that I wasn't restricted to professional practice sessions, and could pl; basketball with friends even when he was not competing. For me, tl emotions I go through in a match are two sides of the same coin. On or side is fear. On the other - love of the game. I choose to focus on tl second side. Love of something always triumphs against fear. Whenev I think about the sport of table tennis and how I love playing the spo and competing, the thought of fear dissipates, and does not enter n mind in any way, even during big competitions.

Thank you for coming on this journey with me. Now go out and enjo the sport. Keep a clear mind when you are competing. Keep yourself the best physical shape possible. Try to find a good balance of practi and resting. Enjoy competing. Keep on fighting. That doesn't mean yo should not try and win, but remember to keep things in perspective. your current mindset different from when you first started playing? Ho has it changed? When we are about to play a table tennis match, thir about why we started playing table tennis in the first place. I have see many players of all levels taking the game a bit too seriously. Try ar relax! Learn to have fun at a tournament. Find enjoyment in yo matches. And when the score is 9-9 in the fifth, enjoy the moment.

Play and fight for the love of the game!

5 TORONTO: PARA PAN AM GAMES

As I mentioned in the introduction of this book, it's been more tha two years since Ping Pong For Fighters was released. In that time, graduated from New York University with a Master of Social Wor studied for and passed the National State Exam to become a License Master of Social Work (LMSW). I have also worked with substance abus clients as well as children with autism and their families. This kind of work was the first time I was doing something outside of table tenn which was very meaningful to me.

Two months after I graduated with an MSW in the summer of 201 I was in the final of the Para Pan Am Games against a very tough play from Mexico. I had many people supporting me in this tournament ar among them was former World Champion Stellan Bengtsson. He was the tournament assisting the USA Para National Team and helping n with match preparation and game tactics along with his wife Ang Bengtsson who would be my match coach through-out the enti competition.

The winner of this match would qualify to represent their country the 2016 Paralympic Games in Brazil. My opponent was ranked #23 the world and I was ranked #8 in the world. Had my opponent won th match he would be going to the Paralympic Games and there would I a good chance that I would not be in attendance because my loss to hi would have cost me ranking points and most likely knocked me out of the top 9 players. This is important because only the top 9 players in m class based on world ranking can qualify for the Paralympic Game There are also two other ways to qualify. The first is winning a gold med in your region. For me it would be winning the Para Pan Am Game The second is to get selected as a wild card; which requires a decidir committee to look at many factors to make their choice. There is m guarantee to be selected as a wild card. Wild cards are selected throug region and not country, so some countries do not have a wild card selection. In other words, if you don't win a gold medal in your region and you are outside the top 9 players in the world, you need a good deal of luck to be selected as an athlete to represent your country in the Paralympic Games.

I normally put on my headphones before these big matches as kind of an escape. But, this time I did not do that. I didn't do that because I wanted to be present. I wanted to experience what I was feeling. I felt very confident. I had met with the USOC Psychologist the night before this match. We talked about having a cue word, a word that would bring me into the present moment. I told her that sometimes when I feel pressure I do not move my feet. She told me that focusing on the ball in my sport might be important as well. So, we decided to use two cue words instead of one to stay focused throughout the match. The words would be "ball" and "feet." That was what I had in my mind before the match. If I got into trouble in any way I would use my cue words to get back into the match.

So, there I was, about to start the match. I had warmed up for 30 minutes; we had done ball selection and racket testing. I was standing alongside my opponent, as we were about to march into the arena. Red curtains surrounded us and it felt quite dark as compared to the playing arena. My opponent was listening to music on his headphones and staring straight ahead. We started walking towards the arena and when we reached it my opponent stepped out and I followed closely behind him. I heard loud cheers from the crowd for both my opponent and myself.

When we got to the table we started the usual warm up. I won the serve and once the match began I served the first ball short topspin to my opponent's forehand using my backhand serve. I attacked one ball to his middle and the next ball to his wide forehand and then finished the point with a down line attack to his backhand. I had been practicing combinations against this opponent. I did visualization before the match and I was about as prepared as I could be for this match. During the match, I kept telling myself "ball, feet." I was playing very well and flowing through the match.

In the first game I had a big lead. My opponent won some points to catch up but I won that game. Then I won the second game. I was up two games to zero and one game away from qualifying for the 2016 Paralympic Games. Then things started to go downhill quickly. My opponent was using long pips on his backhand but he would sometimes flip his racket and use the sponge and attack with his backhand. He also had a very strong forehand attack that I had problems controlling. My opponent started flipping the racket even more, alternating between attacking with his backhand and using his forehand attack to push me off the table. I lost the third game and then the fourth game. I kept telling myself "feet, ball" but nothing was working.

I started to feel like I wanted the match to end. I felt as though I wanted to get off the table as soon as possible and that is not the best feeling to have during a table tennis match. As competitors, we probably should be feeling just the opposite. We should enjoy the match and want the match to go on as long as possible. But, the enjoyment of the match had diminished. I was playing for the result. I erroneously believed that I had to win the match. That if I lost the match it would be terrible. I probably would not qualify for the Paralympic Games and this loss would set off a series of negative events. The assumption that somehow I would lose something as a person had I not won this match was simply a thought that was not reality based.

We started the fifth game and I just could not find a way out of my opponent's combinations. When I attacked, he knocked me out of the point with solid blocks and when he attacked I could not control his forehand. Also, he was messing me up by backhand flipping the racket. Sometimes he would play fast with the backhand and sometimes he would play slow. I had to deal with moving in and out as well as covering his strong forehand attack. At this point in time, nowhere I played on the table was safe for me. I went down 2-5 in the final game. That's when a thought occurred to me.

It occurred to me that this match was over. I started to believe that I could not win the match. It was probably a combination of things. Thinking about the result, giving the match an immense amount of importance and mostly because I believed that losing this match would diminish who I am as a table tennis player and human being. I started to tell myself that it was OK that I lost because I am a social worker. I have a career which is more important than winning table tennis matches. I told myself that after this match I would go home and start a job as a social worker helping others.

This was a big moment for me; and 50% of a lesson that I needed to understand, which I would fully understand one year later. I could finally see something beyond just winning a table tennis match. The other 50% would take place in Rio at the 2016 Paralympic Games because although I was down 5-2 in the final game at the Para Pan Am Games in Toronto I found a way to come back during that match and I won it. I can't say I would have felt OK with the outcome of the match had I lost but once I said to myself that there was something outside of table tennis and table tennis was not the be all and end all, I was halfway to learning what I needed to learn as a competitor and as a person.

At 5-2 down I felt calmer after knowing that table tennis was not everything. At that time, I still hated the fact that I was going to lose the match but I was able to be comfortable in the present moment. Tactically I ended up finding a good combination in the match, which was giving my opponent trouble. Two forehand balls down the line to his backhand and then one ball wide out to his forehand was a very good working combination for me. I lived on that combination and won the final game 11-7. I was only able to do that because I moved out of "results

thinking", I moved out of the future, into the present. At the Paralymp
Games in Rio I would experience a totally different outcome and yet tl
lesson was the other half of what I needed to learn and didn't quite g
at the 2015 Para Pan Am Games after winning the Gold Medal. It wou
turn out to be one of the most important life changing experiences fe
me in my career as a table tennis player and in my daily life as a huma
being.

6 RIO: PARALYMPICS GAMES

It was great to be part of the Rio 2016 Paralympic Games. What an awesome experience! My first Paralympic Games was in 1996 and now here I was 20 years later once again competing with the best players in the world. Although there were many complaints about the conditions of the Paralympic Village, I was enjoying my time immensely. Even though I was living in a small room, there were quite a few mosquitoes, problems with consistent hot water and some other minor issues, I felt very comfortable and very calm.

However, one of the things that bothered me was that there were many reports of stolen items. Some athletes had gone to training only to come back to their room and their luggage was stolen with most of their belongings. The working staff that helped to maintain the rooms as well as the security at the games had to be replaced at least once while I was there because they were taking items as well. The United States Olympic Committee (USOC) ended up hiring security staff for extra safety.

I did come to the games prepared. I went to Home Depot while I was still in the United States and bought many locks to take with me. I locked all of my bags and chained them to the bed in my room where they could not be removed, unless someone decided to carry out the entire bed! I also made sure not to clean any laundry that had USA written on it or hang any laundry outside. One thing I noticed that was quite interesting was the USOC did not display the American Flag on our building. Usually in all the past games they had done that but this time they said because of security it would not be done. They were afraid that we might be attacked.

I arrived at the games early. As a matter a fact, I was at the Paralympic Village eight days before the competition started. I had a lot of time to kill. I did a lot of walking around in the Paralympic Village. I

got a haircut in the village barbershop, booked a tour to see the Christ
Redeemer statue with my coach, team leader and one of my teammate
I also got a chance to do some training in the competition hall and in
the playing venue. The playing conditions at the venue were very good
I did however find that the table tennis table had a weird bounce and
the balls were not the all that good but they were OK.

So, after all my training, resting and hanging around the Paralympic
Village it was finally time to compete. The draw was out and my draw
was quite tough. I had the defending Paralympic Gold Medalist who
was from China in my group and I also had the number one Hungaria
Class 9 player in my group. Hungary and China would play first. That
match order provided me with a great opportunity to watch my two
opponents battle against each other. I watched the match and took
notes. China ended up winning against Hungary in three close tight
games.

The next day I played against the defending Paralympic Gold
Medalist from China. I felt good going into the match because we had
played two years earlier in the semis of the Slovakia Para Open and I
had won against him 3-2. I knew that he might be thinking about the
prior match. I started the first game with a good lead. I was playing we
and I was very patient. I then began to rush things and before I knew i
I went down 0-3 in games. It was not the best feeling to lose 0-3 in
games mainly because I had rushed the match and before the match I
told myself I would take my time each and every point. I told myself
that the longer the match went on the more enjoyable it would be. I
failed to follow my own advice, rushing through the match and feeling
uncomfortable competing.

The good news however was that two players would advance from
the group into the next round. If I could win my next round I would b
able to get out of the group. However, this was not an easy task. The
Hungarian player was tough. I had first played against him at the Worl

Championships in 2002 where I was down 8-4 in the final game and rallied back to win 14-12. We had played 4 times after that match and I won three times and he won once. The last time we played at the Slovenia Open in the Team Event in 2014, he had beaten me.

What was strange about that match was that I played so well and still lost. But, I had taken notes on that match after my loss and in my notes, I saw that I lost because I had played the balls to fast and had given him too much speed. This time my plan was to do the opposite. I had planned to give him nothing to work with. I would only play the ball fast when I was in a good position I would also place the ball in a way that would be difficult for him, hitting off speed shots and attacking his middle forehand.

I stuck to my tactics and ended up winning the match. I won three games to zero. The first game I had a big lead and he was catching up but I was able to close it out. The second game I won quite easily and the third game I won 11-7. The tactics had worked. I would now be advancing to the single elimination stage!

My coach and team leader went to the draw meeting to find out who my next opponent would be. In the meantime, I waited in my room for a few hours for the draw to be complete. Later, I ended up meeting the team at an outdoor cafe inside the Paralympic Village. My first single elimination match would be against the top player from France. This was going to be a big challenge for me. This guy was previously on the French able-bodied team. He had a very stable backhand and strong tactics. Furthermore, he had knocked me out of the group stage at the London 2012 Paralympics 3-1 in games. It was a tough loss.

Three days prior to getting the single elimination draw I was walking with my coach We had just finished a practice and we wanted to check out the main stadium. On the way, there we had run into the French player. He was heading towards the athlete lounge. He was walking with a girl who appeared to be his daughter. She was probably about four years old and was carrying a table tennis racket. She seemed to be quite excited to be walking down the hall and just spending time with her father. It was pretty cool to see. I told my coach that if I should play this French player in the tournament, it would be near impossible to beat him if his daughter was coaching the match. She exhibited such a high level of wonderment and curiosity just being in the Paralympic Village; she should probably get a medal just for showing up.

I started the next day off well. Got a good warm up, ate two apples, watched some video of my opponent and prepared myself mentally for the match. So, there I was about to face off against a great player who was probably one level better than I was. But, like I mentioned earlier in this book; a table tennis match is not about who is better. It is about how is better on that day or rather during the match. I didn't need to be better than my opponent all the time. I just had to find a way to be better during our match. The only way I was going to do that was to play smart, work hard and fight for every ball.

My opponent and I walked in together to the umpire and officials ball selection and match preparation room. My opponent looked quite confident. We selected the ball, made sure we had two different color shirts on and then went to an area where the officials would cover up most of our logos, because in the Paralympic Games we can only have one logo showing. I then sat down and waited for our match to be called.

We walked out together into the stadium after waiting for what seemed like two hours. We started the warm up. I was moving OK and I felt good. When I played this guy in London at the Paralympics I lost 3-1 and he just killed me with the backhand. His backhand control was outstanding and he uses his backhand covering probably 80% of the table. I decided that I would have to find a way to get the ball to his forehand more and that is exactly what I did during the first game but his forehand started playing so well. He was making so many strong forehand attacks. I lost the first game 6-11.

It really wasn't looking very good for me. This guy was controlling my entire game. Nothing I did seemed to bother him. He was trying to move me around the table so he could play a strong attack and I was trying to push him off the table so I could get better angles. He wasn't so strong when he was off the table. I got lucky in the second game and won it. My opponent missed two forehand attacks and I got a net and an edge during two different points winning 11-9. In the third game my opponent started being more aggressive and won easily 11-5. The fourth game we were tied 6-6 and then the dynamics of the match changed.

At 6-6 I was about to start serving and my opponent started saying that my backhand serve was illegal. Something about that call bothered me. So, I started working even harder in the match. My backhand serve is very basic and really doesn't give me any advantage. It's a low short serve and usually my opponents can't really do too much to the serve. I thought to myself that maybe in this match my opponent was uncomfortable with the game being so close. I started pushing myself beyond what I could do. I started moving more. I started working and hustling more on every single point. I won the fourth game 11-8.

In the fifth game I got a very bad start. My opponent started once again playing very aggressively. Before I knew it, I was down 5-9 and serving. I served with my backhand short to the forehand. The ball was returned with a deep push down the line to my backhand. I made a backhand loop down the line and won the point. (I always like to play the first ball down the line or to the middle because it opens the table for me and makes it difficult for my opponent). Next point I served with the backhand again, opened to the middle, my opponent made a counter loop to my backhand. I smashed with the backhand to his middle. He returned the ball. I smashed again to the middle with my backhand and he returned the ball again. Then I used my backhand smash to his backhand and he returned again. Then I used my backhand smash to his wide backhand and won the point.

I was now down 7-9 and I got a bit lucky. My opponent missed two balls to his middle on his forehand side. For some reason, he was having trouble playing a strong ball from the middle of the table, slightly to his forehand. I focused only on that position and played most of the balls there for the remainder of the match. I won that game 11-9. It was a great comeback. I felt bad after the match because it was so devastating for my opponent. He just sat in a chair stunned. I had stopped him from his chance of winning a Paralympic Gold Medal in Brazil 2016 just as he had stopped me in London 2012.

When I used to play years ago, and I was much younger I just had this thought all the time of killing my opponent. I wanted to totally destroy them no matter who I played. I looked at the person on the opposite side of the table as an obstacle, as someone who was standing in the way of my championship. I saw myself as a champion and I used to think, "Who is this person that is trying to stand in the way of my championship?" So, there was this relationship in my own mind of myself as a "champion" and of my opponent as kind of "subhuman." There was no thought at that time that this person is just like me. They want to win the match and the championship also.

I didn't make too many friends during that time because I hated the people I was competing against, but after I started college in 2006 my view began to change. I started to develop relationships with my opponents that were not just about competing. I started to develop friendships with them. I began to see another side of who they are. I think my perception changed at that time because I was no longer a fulltime Table Tennis player. Table Tennis wasn't everything for me. I started to see that I had other things in my life but I still had a lot to learn about putting these things into the proper perspective. Competing is great, but table tennis is not bigger than life.

I was now in the quarterfinals of the Paralympic Games in Brazil. If I could get through this match I would be in the medal round. I was up against the number one player from Belgium. He was having some very good results lately. He had won the Para European Championships and was currently the number one able-bodied junior in Belgium. He was left-handed which was good for me because my style works very well against left handed players. It's very tough for a left-handed player to get away from my backhand.

This match was a bit different than my previous three matches. This time I wasn't feeling that good going into the match. (My first match of the day was against Hungary and that was at 9:00am). Stellan Bengtsson told me that in Sweden they had done many studies of athlete peak performance. In one of the studies they determined that an athlete's body is not fully awake until they have been awake for three hours. They did this by having Swedish National Team Members play matches one hour after they woke up, two hours after they woke up and three hours after they woke up. They found that the player who had been awake for at least 3 hours would win the most matches. They also found that the player who had been awake for less time would typically lose their matches. One of the reasons they could reach these conclusions was because they were having the same people play against each other. One player would play the match after being awake for one hour and then the next day the same player would play the same opponent but this time would be awake for three hours.

That being said, I woke up at 5:30am for a 9:00am match. Which was the correct thing to do. Then I had a 4:00pm match which was extremely tough. Now I was getting ready for an 8:00pm match. My coach Angie Bengtsson and I continued with the same preparation as previous matches. We had a great warm up and I felt OK during the match but this time I did not win the match. The first and third games were very close. I had a lot of trouble with his short forehand serve and

101

I got unlucky on some critical points.

After I lost in the quarterfinals something happened that had never happened to me in any match I have ever played over my twenty plus years as a professional table tennis athlete. I felt comfortable with the loss. Of course, I wanted to win but I was OK with losing. I tried my best and did all I could to win. That's all we can hope for when we compete. I kind of had that feeling throughout the games; no matter what the result I would probably be comfortable with it because I did all I could in my preparation. That is exactly what happened. I was totally comfortable with the result but most importantly I felt that the loss could no way diminish my "ok-ness" as a person.

The player I lost to in the quarterfinals is a good competitor. He has wins over two of our USA National Team Members and as I write this he is at the World Junior Championships and just played a match against our USA Olympian and Current National Champion Kanak Jha at the World Junior Championships. I sent Kanak a video one-day prior to the match explaining what it was like to play against the number one Para player from Belgium and gave a few tips in the video. Kanak ended up winning the match 4-0: 12-10, 11-9, 13-11 and 13-11! Hopefully Kanak will be able to send me some tips and advice when I play against the Belgian player again in the future.

I forgot to mention this earlier but in Rio I spoke with the National Team Coach of the player I had beaten from Mexico at the 2015 Para Pan Am Games. I was told that the player had quit the sport of table tennis because of his loss to me. I remember feeling bad after the match in 2015 because my opponent broke down crying. It was a great opportunity for him to qualify for his first Paralympic Games. It would have been a very good win for him. During our match in the fifth game he started to rush a bit towards the end of that game. He may have been thinking about the result of the match and rushing to finish the match as soon as possible.

When I heard from his coach that he quit table tennis, I thought "that's really too bad." I hope he will come back to the sport. He is a great player and a great competitor, but whether he comes back or not I hope he will learn the lesson that took me over 20 years to learn. Win or lose, I am never in deficit as a human being. Winning doesn't define who I am and neither does losing. Sure, it feels amazing to win a great match or championship but really in my own life nothing changes. If I win or lose I can still practice social work, I can still eat food and I can still play table tennis. Life remains the same. The Rio Paralympics are over and there is always another tournament to try and compete and enjoy and be part of.

I think it's ironic that Kanak Jha's opponent in the 2016 North American Olympic Qualifier who leading 5-0 in the final game against Kanak ended up quitting the sport after the result of that match. Kanak came back and won the final game 11-5 after being down 0-5. This result caused the Canadian player to officially retire from table tennis in a very similar way as my opponent when I qualified for Rio. Dealing with this type of pressure seems like an ongoing challenge in the sport of table tennis today. One of my goals in writing this book was to provide insight on how to manage this type of self-induced pressure. The best way I know how to do that is to reduce the importance of the match and know that the result of the match does not define who I am.

I am going to end by saying that in sport and in life it's been my experience that if you want to achieve a goal; go out and take a chance. Never fear failure and never be afraid to fail. You have more to lose if you don't try than if you try and fail. When I finished a Master's of Social Work in 2015 the next step for me was to take the Master of Social Work State Exam so that I could get a license and practice social work ad an LMSW. I had just gotten out of school and all the material for the exam was still very fresh in my mind but I did not take the exam right away. I kept putting it off thinking that I needed to prepare more.

I would tell myself that in four weeks I would take the exam and I would even schedule the date of the exam, only to cancel that date and postpone it another four weeks. I did this for more than six months.

In the month of November 2015 I had once again made plans to take the state exam. I had a Team Tournament during Thanksgiving Weekend and I scheduled the exam one-week prior. However, two day before the exam day I rescheduled the exam again for December 9th 2016. I once again thought I needed more time.

My coach Sean O'Neill with whom I speak with daily realized there was a problem. We spoke in detail about the exam. I told him that I didn't think I was ready to take it and I needed more time. Sean convinced me to take it. He said that even if I failed it would be an opportunity to embrace failure in a positive way and I could always tak the exam again in another few months. One of the most important things he stressed has to do with information.

Sean's logic was that even if I had failed the test I would have had more information than if I had not taken the exam at all. When we los a match in table tennis we can use that information to help us better prepare for when we play that same opponent again. The same logic applies when taking an exam. I would know what it would be like to take the exam. I could use that experience to help me in case I had to take it again.

I took his advice and took the exam. I not only passed but also received an extremely high score. So, the point I am trying to make with all of this is that we never really know what is going to happen. There are events in our lives that are uncontrollable. I have no control over whether I can pass an exam. I have no control over whether I cai win a table tennis match or a tournament but if I do not enter the tournament then I certainly have no chance to win it. The same goes for taking an exam. Many times, we spend our lives not doing something because of the uncertainty of the result but in reality, result don't define who we are. Those are just external things. We define who we are and we do it by trying to do the best we can each day, each hour and each moment.

I want to thank you for taking the time to read this book. I tried my very best to write a book that was clear and concise. My main goal for this book was so that athletes and coaches could see the sport of table tennis in a different way and that they could challenge and question themselves: so, that they can understand that sport in itself is a learning process.

I don't think that I am going to write another book like this one again because I feel that this book reached the level of what I was trying to do. I am completely satisfied with how this version came out and I am not sure I can do much better. I have been working on a table tennis autobiography that I will probably release and if I do it will be out in the summer of 2017. Be well, train hard and never give up.

Tahl Leibovitz

ACKNOWLEDGEMENTS

I would like to thank the following people for making this Gold Med edition book possible: My wife Dawn Leibovitz, My twin sister Maja Leibovi Cecilia Leibovitz, Sean O' Neill, Estee Ackerman, Guy Kuperman, Don Torre M.D., Dov Kolker M.D., Stellan and Angie Bengtsson. I would also li to thank my team mate Mitch Seidenfeld.

ABOUT THE AUTHOR

Tahl Leibovitz started playing table tennis at the South Queens Boys Club in New York City when he was 14 years old. A Paralympic gold medalist, Tahl has won over 125 major championships and titles. Tahl has completed degrees in Philosophy and Sociology from Queens College (CUNY) as well as a Master's degree in Urban Studies. In 2015 Tahl completed a Master's of Social Work degree from New York University Silver School of Social Work, and then passed the New York State LMSW Licensing Examination. Tahl would eventually like to open a table tennis center for marginalized individuals offering table tennis instruction and psychotherapy. Tahl lives in Queens, New York with his wife and two dogs.

1589- 142

PROJECT TABLE TENNIS

Project Table Tennis is a team oriented company which operat nationally throughout the United States implementing, managing or supportii a series of ongoing projects centered around communities and families. Ma of our projects combine Table Tennis and Social Work as a vehicle to he foster meaningful relationships between people. Project Table Tennis address Alzheimer's, Dementia, Veterans with Disabilities, Drug & Alcohol Abuse well as Obesity by serving seniors, youth, children and addicted populations.

- Supportive Programs for Assisted Living & Senior Centers
- Table Tennis Programs in Public & Private Schools
- Adaptive Workshops for Veterans with Disabilities
- Table Tennis Lessons & Camps
- Table Tennis Equipment
- Public Speaking
- Ratings Central

Please visit our website: www.projecttabletennis.com

Made in United States
Troutdale, OR
10/25/2024

24120775R10067